Acknowledgements

When you make a transi͟ _ _ ͟ as far and deep into hell as I've come from there is no way that you do it alone. Nor is there truly anyway to acknowledge every single person that played a significant role in your growth. Therefore, if you were involved in this journey with me I thank you and you and I both know the love that is there.

However, I want to give a shout out to my daughter A'myah Parson (Princess My My) and my son De'Vonte' Parson II. You two mean the world to me and I dedicate every part of my being to ensure you won't have to, at least without prior warning, go through the pain and suffering I put myself through.

People who did time with me:

Omari, Tori, Shay, D-Folks, Nit-Nit, Treya, Amber, K.K., Mom, B. Hostile, Estaban…and those I didn't add I never forgot you fam!

People who mentored me:

Unc, Chris, Peep, Brother Michael, G.P., O.J., Big Munch & Momma Candace, Jamaica, Rellioso, Ms. Beckham, Lucas, Cindy, Barbara, Jacob, Pat, William, J. Nova, Gooooooey Oooey, Stevie da P Dicky, Ron G, Estaban….and so many more!

Also,

R.I.P. M.C. although you were unable to shake those demons once released I still knew you and saw you as a great man which you will forever be in my eyes King!

Treasure Chest

BECOMING

THE MANIFESTERS (THE INTRODUCTION):

"Painful as it may be, a significant emotional event can be the catalyst for choosing a direction that serves us - and those around us - more effectively. Look for the learning."

Louisa May Alcott

The purpose of this book is not to give you any sort of biography about who I am as an individual nor is it to place myself on any sort of high horse because I was able to outgrow my circumstances and become more. The potential in myself is the same potential you have in yourself. My goal is to motivate you to evolve as an individual into the person you truly want to become. I know it sounds cliché' but the truth is if I can do it YOU definitely can do it. I was a young, dumb, broke gang member who was in special education and had no hopes of a future whatsoever. Look at who I have become now and where I plan to take this

These lessons I've learned have been broken down into chapters called "Jewels" that are precise and concise so that you yourself can take them and immediately apply them to bring Treasure into your life. These lessons have worked for me and every single one may not work for you. However, try them out and see what the results are. There are different levels of growth and I understand that trust me. Therefore, you can skip ahead in this book to where you are on your journey which is why I segmented them in "Becoming, Living It, and Being" which are the three phases in the evolution of life in my opinion. "Becoming" is to take away old beliefs, ways, and habits so that you can start anew. "Living It" is to replace those old beliefs, ways, and habits with the ones you need to evolve and placing those new habits into practice. Lastly, "Being" is to build on what foundation you've laid out for yourself and allowing those who may have not yet taken the leap to learn from you. Please give yourself a chance and put the principles to play in this book. Oh, I almost forgot that I placed a section for an action plan at the end of every jewel for you to reflect on how you will put what you have just learned into action. Come with me and lets Manifest.

May 15, 2015, around two o'clock in the morning would become the night that changed my life. As weird as it may sound the Ultimate change was intentional but the catalyst to create it was not. Without boring you with specific details I will give you a summary of the event.

I was dating a girl that I wasn't supposed to be in the first place because she was my good friend's long time ex-girlfriend. She and I were both off of work that day and decided to drink a bottle of Remy to the neck then hit up our other friends to plan somewhere to go for the night. We found our friends, for namesake we'll call them O and Bre, ready to go out and party to celebrate O getting accepted into the Electricians apprenticeship. We met up at their apartment, got poo face drunk, and headed out to a bar in Tacoma, Wa is known for its shootings and gang attendance. SMH, so here we all were drunk as skunks, driving while playing Mozzy, and oh, did I mention O and I both had our loaded guns in the car. I'm with a girl I'm not supposed to be with, driving a car I shouldn't be driving at my level of inebriation, and headed to a place I shouldn't be going. It doesn't' take a rocket scientist to see that something was really about to go down. Which it did…..

O and I are in the club getting drunk with the girls and having the time of our lives. All of us being from Seattle, Washington we have a natural incline to be boisterous and loud which we did to the fullest. Some guys didn't take a liking to that and approached O asking him about his gang affiliation. Mind you, O doesn't bang he's just a thorough street dude. After giving his answer the two men were not satisfied and continued pronging. I became fed up and punched one in the face inciting a riot in there. Now here we all are drunk, fighting against a club of gang members in a place where we are not familiar. DUMB. After the rumble, I walk outside with my girl at the time to find O because we had been split by security during the altercation. He was leaning in the car and when he got out he had his gun in hand headed to the bar. I followed suit and grabbed mines as well. We started shooting, people started screaming and before I knew it I was in handcuffs laying on my side with a tazor prong stuck in my ribs. Did I mention I had pissed on myself from the multiple tazor shocks? They hooked and booked me for what would be Eight Assault in the First Degrees, a Drive-By Shooting, and Unlawful Possession of a Firearm. Bail was set at a half-million dollars and my fight for my life and the opportunity to see the streets again began there. Afraid, Lost and Confused was the boy facing the rest of his natural life in prison. However, it began my transformation into a man, Follow ME....

3 plead not guilty in a drive-by shooting outside Tacoma bar

BY STACIA GLENN - STAFF WRITER

MAY 19, 2015 11:10 AM, UPDATED MAY 19, 2015 11:17 AM

A drive-by shooting early Saturday outside a Tacoma bar might have been retaliation for a fight earlier in the night but the victims weren't part of the earlier brawl, according to court records.

No one was injured in the shooting, which happens at about 1:10 a.m. in the 8400 block of South Hosmer Street.

Three people were charged.

Omari Brown, 24, of Kent, and Devonte Parson, 22, of Federal Way, pleaded not guilty Monday to four counts of first-degree assault, drive-by shooting, and first-degree unlawful possession of a firearm. Bail was set at $500,000 for each.

BECOMING

Jewel #1: Do What YOU Have to Do…Now

"Do for yourself what nobody else is going to do for you; like you."

- Don Cherry

I had a conversation with my public defender in July 2015 asking him about what deals would be on the table that didn't require becoming some sort of confidential informant. He informed me that he had not yet been able to even begin looking over my case at that point and therefore couldn't give me the slightest idea on what may be offered. I was furious because I had been sitting in the county jail for almost three months confused, worried, and damn near at the point of giving up and this man hadn't even gone over my paperwork yet. I hung up the phone but not without him begrudgingly agreeing to hit the prosecutor up immediately and see what the state may be offering. Bad move, two days later I got a letter in the mail stating "De' Vonte' Parson is in a lot of trouble and I have enough evidence to convict him already. Therefore, my first and only offer is 240 mos. For the Assault in the First degrees and a 5-year gun enhancement that is to be served consecutively with no early release to earn. Please remind your client that he is in a lot of trouble and if he fights this and loses we will push for the maximum penalty which will result in a life sentence outright. Thank You."

I fell out on my bunk with that paper in my hand and didn't come out of that funk for at least three days. I hadn't felt so helpless in my life since watching my grandmother being taken out of our home in handcuffs as a kid and me not being able to do anything about it. The system had me where they wanted me and I was now defenseless...or so I thought.

After about the third day of depression in that cell, stressed the hell out about the entire situation my homeboy Snoop came in and checked on me. "Aye bruh you all F'd up behind that offer but damn what can you do about it but wait?" he asked in what was an attempt at helping me feel better. I just looked at him with no expression at all. "Well, I did hear about a dude going prose' like O.G. in here. That stuff is hella risky and hard. They feel like they got you then, but the dude said it worked best for his case. I got a book on it written by someone who did it and succeeded also if you want to read it." Snoop shrugged his shoulders and left. He hadn't known that he had just sparked a fight in me that even I had not known was there up until that point. The next day, after thinking about the idea for a second, I had the book in my possession detailing how to begin as a prose' defendant and I called my lawyer and fired him just like that. We sat up a court date with the judge asking me a few questions about my mental health and before I knew it I was now my own attorney. The crazy part is now that I think about it, I clearly had to have some sort of mental health issues to commit the crime that I did in the nature that it was done but I think they were like who cares he's cooked anyway. Today I can laugh looking back and say "think again."

Hidden Jewel:

We're all faced with those moments in life where we can choose to take action or let things be. I believe that far too many of us take the latter option either out of **Ignorance**, **Laziness**, or **Fear**. Each of those things can be alleviated by just taking back control.

Ignorance is pretty much lacking the knowledge of a particular subject. That means that once you study up on whatever it is and learn the fundamentals, place what you learned into practice and you are no longer ignorant. The sad part is many choose to stay ignorant because of our next two killers. Of taking control: Laziness and Fear.

I was ignorant of anything about law besides being on the losing end of it until I caught my case and chose to take the fight into my own hands. Once I overcame the fear and laziness, which I will explain how in a second, and decided to put hours into studying the law I was no longer ignorant.

Therefore, when choosing to take control of a situation study and learn all of the fundamentals for you to move accordingly to do what you have to do.

Laziness is not having the motivation to do something although you have the ability to do so. I watched so many guys inside who were far more intelligent than myself go ahead and let the public pretenders do what they wanted with their case because they refused to go to the law library or read books and figure out how to win. These guys often spoke on how they were going to start looking, or how they wanted to, etc. etc. However, none of them ever followed through and some actually still ended up in favorable positions. Though much more were played and tossed somewhere in the system never to be found again.

I was able to sit down and share meals with the man accused of playing a part in killing those four Lakewood police officers. I won't comment on the legalities of his case or what I may know about his innocence and how he may be being held under political matters rather than the truth of conviction. What I will say is that man stayed studying and fighting for his freedom. He used almost every waking hour doing what he could to get his life back.

That's the way you must go about getting after whatever it is you want in this life. Laziness will give no room for success. The two cannot live together and one must go. There were times when I didn't feel like going to the law library and studying just because I was so depleted. However, I would just get up and walk out of the cage. By doing that action I was locked in and committed to the play. After that, each step was a little easier honestly.

Sometimes, you just have to get up and walk out of the cage to commit and the action will eat away at the laziness I promise.

Fear is like the serial killer of all great dreams and ambitions but especially in taking action. Man, an entire book can be written on fear alone and some actually have. However, fear is the unproven feeling that something unpleasant could or MAY happen. Therefore, there isn't any real substance to fear but what we make of it in our own minds. The thing about it is things usually never turn out how we feared it would and we end up stressing for no reason.

There were many times I experienced fear and had to move forward while in that situation. The biggest one was actually deciding to defend the case myself in the first place when facing a life sentence if I failed. Mind you I had never been to trial, couldn't remember the last time I read a book, and knew nothing about law at all besides pleading guilty. Trust me fear reminded me of those things all the way up until my decision. Fear also used others like my Fiance at the time to question what I was doing. Yeah, it will attack you through those closest to really get your attention.

How I learned to conquer fear was to attack whatever I had head-on. There was a philosophy I took on in the streets called "F**k IT". Where if I felt scared to do anything from an all-out brawl to a potential shooting I'd shut off my be=rain to anything that would stop me and immediately act. By the time my mind opened back up I was already committed and in action. When I sat at that phone contemplating going prose' I just shut my mind down, called, and sat the date. By doing that you don't give the fear time to respond because you shut down for that small window of time. Remember, you only have maybe a three-second window before the opportunity is over so be quick in your action.

Therefore, if you want to take back control to do what you have to for yourself say "F It" and jump in. Fear won't be able to follow you if you move fast enough.

Who Must You Become?

INSIGHT

I remember as a kid I had one hell of an imagination. Shit, sometimes I used to imagine my dad coming back alive and seeing me for the first time rescuing me from the projects...but that never happened. On a more serious note, I used to imagine myself being different heroes in my mind. However, the heroes were not your typical batman and superman characters that come across as pure and void of any evil. My hero did have evil in him yet he was still able to do some good, fighting other bad guys that came around. Looking back I think I got that from the older kids in the neighborhood who were looked at by society as "thugs" who would rob you or disgusting "gang members" who may kill you. To me and the other little kids in the neighborhood, they were big brothers who would give you a couple of bucks when you were down because your grandmother was sick and couldn't work to provide a stable income. They were protectors who would keep other neighborhood bullies from coming in and attacking us vulnerable kids. Anyways, I was weird and used to become these weird creatures in mind to the point I damn near believed they were really me. Therefore, when I realized I went prose' the next thought was "Well, damn now I have to become a damn lawyer." It was on from there.

What I learned when transitioning into who you want to be you must learn who you must become. If you want to become a businessman well get your butt into the mindset of a businessman. If you want to become a professor you better start thinking like a damn professor. If you want to be a boss in your neighborhood you better start acting like a boss in your neighborhood. Whatever it is you want to be you have to figure out what you must become.

"You must Be before you can Do something" was said by John Gielgud. I don't know exactly what role he played in this crazy world however I do know that he was wise enough to speak that truth to power. The act of first Being is magic in itself. When you act out the traits of whatever it is that you want to become in advance then your brain develops the waves to actually transform your entire persona. I once heard from a great speaker Jim Cathcart that "If you want to be an oak tree think like an oak tree, because if you continue thinking like an acorn you'll remain an acorn." At each court appearance, I was perceived as intelligent, well-spoken, and savvy. The reason being is because when I wasn't in court if I wasn't pouring over my case looking for holes in the prosecutor's story I was reading John Grisham books (a retired lawyer turned author) attempting to get into the mind of a lawyer all the way down to how they saw things and spoke. I was looking through other people's cases and asking them how their court appearances went in detail so that I can gain an understanding of the procedures. I would walk around the tank reciting my opening and closing statements so I wouldn't be in fear of speaking it in front of the jury. I did all of those things in an attempt to become a lawyer because it was who I HAD to become. You have to take that same approach when pursuing whoever it is you want to become. BE before you can Do and Have.

Dig For Gold:

My goal in this book is not only for you to read but to provoke some active evolution within yourself. I want to take you through the process I went through to have the transformation I experienced. Therefore, take these small projects extremely seriously for us both. Let's dig a little into what you actually want and who it is that you really want to become. Even if you feel as if you are who you planned to be there are still more levels to go my friend.

If you could sum up the Vision for your life in a small paragraph what would it look like? (Please dream big because it's the only effective way of dreaming that has given the world progress.)?

What character traits does the person who carries that vision have to hold to build and maintain it? Which ones do you still need to work on building into yourself right now?

What will you start working on today that will go towards evolving the character that is necessary for tomorrow?

Raise Your Self-Expectations

Insight

My grandmother raised me and always reminds me of how annoying I was as a youth. I remember certain instances she speaks of however others are a bit more blurry. I can't deny the fact that to this day even my own kids say that I get on their nerves sometimes when I pinch their cheeks, or jump on the bed and make them bounce to wake them up and I even tickle them TOO much. Now, how and the hell do you tickle a kid TOO much? Yeah, I can be that annoying. In a brain class I took in prison it said when you get excitement from irritating others there's actually a certain part of your brain that has not been developed fully (shrugs) I guess. Anyways, my grandmother said that since she could remember I would be called a pest by everyone because of my annoyances. One day into my pre-teen years I was bothering her like usual and she asked me "why are you so annoying De'Vonte.'" Without hesitation, I told her it was because I was a pest. Now it may seem harmless but think how I had been programmed most of my life to believe that I was a pest. Though I was, it is still proof that what people put on you and you agree with while you're young will earn a spot as truth in your head. What have you been conditioned to take on as truth?

I once did a Facebook live and youtube video encouraging people to raise their expectations for themselves. This was inspired by listening to a build by Tony Robbins where he was discussing how people build these grand goals and don't believe they could ever actually accomplish them. He went on to explain that there's no point in setting a goal that you don't even believe you can accomplish because you'll sabotage yourself in pursuit of it.

Reflecting on his wise words I realized that most of our expectations of self begin with how we were perceived as kids and how we perceive ourselves now. We become exactly who we think we are. When you're a child, especially one who comes from poverty certain expectations are cast upon you. A young man is expected to become a Drug dealer, Gang member, or Inmate. A young lady is expected to become a Prostitute, Young single Mother, or Section 8 recipient. Even if the world doesn't verbally communicate these expectations to you they inform you of them in other ways such as their interactions when your paths and theirs cross from time to time. You don't even have to come from poverty you can grow up in a wealthy and healthy environment yet are told you are dumb or a loser by the people who surrounded you as a child.

What happens is that kid grows to fit these "jackets" that have been placed on him or her and they expect that of themselves. They gradually travel through life with these false beliefs about themselves and are hindered because of them.

On my journey to becoming a "lawyer" to fight my case, I had to overcome certain expectations that I had of myself that were negative. One was that I was too stupid to do it because I had been in special ed classes my entire life. I can laugh at it now but I remember in high school even though my associates and I had all the girls and were popular, behind our backs they called us the "Special Ed Gangsters." Where the hell they do that at? I had to remind myself while fighting this case that I was not dumb and the work was actually fairly easy for me it was my behavior that was the problem. That was exactly the case now. All that I had to do was control my temper when communicating with this prosecutor and remain disciplined in my studies despite all of the distractions in jail. The bookwork would be easy because despite what they believed I was actually smart.

Therefore, I encourage you to dive into your expectations of yourself. Find out which ones are positive and which are negative. You determine that by pairing them with which ones are conducive to who you need to become and which are not. The expectations that are not to your liking, if you can, flip them just like I did the stupid to smart. However, if they are just downright negative you have to do away with them. The only way that you will be successful in your endeavors is if you truly expect yourself to be. Et The Hip Hop Preacher said, "Some of you are living under beliefs about yourselves that aren't even true anymore." You have likely grown out of many things that were expected of you at some point yet you're still holding it true to heart. It's an outdated time to upgrade and Expect a better you.

Dig For Gold:

There are likely expectations you placed on yourself or that was placed on you long ago that you have now outgrown, what may they be? Do your best to find at least three to attack and become more.

Jump All In

Insight

I remember it was 2005 when I first got put on the neighborhood by a friend of mines I had just met maybe two months prior. I was twelve years old and felt that if I wanted to be respected I had to choose up with a block in the community. All of my friends were already choosing up with other gangs and it was becoming unsafe to not be able to claim your hood when someone asked you "where you from?" I chose 31st and E. Cherry St. because it was something being revived as a gang and wasn't saturated by a bunch of false claimers and what not. I believed that if I went hard enough for an up and coming hood then it would go in the history books of the gangsters. I didn't realize how naive of a belief that was at the time because at the end of the day nobody is remembered for more than 20 years, at least not significantly. Back to my point, I remember sitting in my project apartment looking in the mirror holding the first black bandana I've ever had. I wrapped it around my face and decided from that point on I was all in and nothing else mattered.

Once you have figured out who it is you must become and you're ready to become, you have to make that conscious decision that no matter what comes with it you will be all in for the cause. That means that there are no shortcuts or easy routes to what you want to do. You will not give up in times of adversity nor will you stand down when it's time to stand up. There has to be a certain glue to your thinking for you to stick with it.

Ray Bradbury once said "jump and you will find out how to unfold your wings as you fall." Many of us feel that we have to know every detail of a particular situation to make a decision. We want to know every possibility in pursuit of a goal. We feel we must be an expert in something to launch a business. MESSAGE, you will never know everything to make a 100% bet that you will be successful in whatever aspect. I once read that successful people only need 60% - 80% of the information to make whatever decisions they must make. Figure out what you know and use it. The rest will figure itself out as long as you take John C. Maxwell's advice and "Fail early, fail often, and fail forward."

What is it right now that you're putting off doing because you feel as if you're not yet ready? F that and go Do IT! Go out on a limb with a mind of "What I do know I'll use and what I don't know I'll learn on the way." There are too many individuals out there that are willing to do right now what you want and are fighting for the same spot that you are. If you don't get at it now guess who the race goes to....the hungriest.

As I was fighting my own case there were plenty of times that I wanted to throw in the towel. The prosecutor was making it difficult for me to receive every document I needed to fight my case. I watched other people who were doing what I was get cooked and laughed at for trying it. My ex-girlfriend was telling me that her lawyer was even saying that I was a fool and would ruin the entire case sending everyone to prison forever. However, I kept pushing through it all. What kept me going was a book in the Bible. Nehemiah was the book to be exact. It was inspirational because the book pushed faith through actions. I won't spoil the book here but when you read it I want you to notice that not once did Nehemiah pray and wait for God's answers via words. Every time he prayed he got up and started moving. I based my entire fight on that book in the bible and I implore you to do the same. Pray and jump in expecting to learn on the way.

It's All a Gamble Anyways

Insight

I remember the month vividly just not the exact date. It was July 2016. I had been in the county jail fighting my case Prose' tooth and nail for 14 Mos. Now, Everyone including the prosecutor had finally come to respect my movement. My girlfriend at the time had one of the top lawyers to represent her and he would come down give me kudos and teach me how to get better. He had even suggested I would have made a great attorney in another life. Anyways, everyone was about to go to the court to produce our closing arguments. This is where it mattered the most. Everyone could respect my intelligence and all but if I couldn't convince the jury to sway in my direction it was over. My life would be spent in a closed custody prison somewhere until I grew gray hairs and died. A great sized burden to be on a 22-year-old kids shoulders huh?

My standby counsel approached me before the jurors came in and said "Mr. Parson you could stop this all right here right now. We can say you underrepresented yourself and you didn't know what it was that you were doing. The case would have to start over but you could get qualified legal representation. Your life hangs in the balance right now. What do you think?" He patiently awaited my answer. "What was the last deal he offered?" I looked at the older gentlemen and asked. He looked at me inquisitively as if he were confused like he didn't let me know before.

"It was 25 Years. That was his only offer since the beginning of this case, Mr. Parson." "And it hasn't changed unless I agree to tell on my co-defendant?" The standby counsel shook his head no. I neatly organized my closing argument notes and looked at him and said "25 years sounds like life to me. I may as well keep up the fight it's a life gamble regardless." The man didn't say it but through his smile, I could tell that he was proud of me standing on my own. We walked through the court doors and I put my dukes up.

After everything is said and done it is all a gamble. Every decision you make is really nothing but a bet since you can never be 100% sure that you'll succeed. The goal is to have the odds in your favor to take calculated risks. Do your due diligence and make it happen. Don't enter this thing with any expectancies besides the fact that no matter what you're going to find your success at some point and somehow.

Once you fixate in your mind that this path is going to make me successful and it's the only way to go you're setting yourself up for possible disappointment. Understand that it's like a poker hand. Every deal is a winner until the flop shows up then the real hands are brought forth. However, once you called pre-flop you know that there was a chance you could lose therefore you made sure that more odds were in your favor than not. That's how you approach the situations when you're chasing after anything you want.

"Life is a gamble there are no sureties. If you want something badly, you'd have to trust your heart and your instincts and take a leap of faith" said Alyssa Urbano. Look you may not trust my word entirely just yet but if you have other people already in successful positions saying the same things then I can't be lying. Take what you know and jump all in with it understanding that a part of you may be lost while doing it. However, if you lose you can learn and come back from it.

When I went prose' and fought it all the way to the end I envisioned that there was a chance that I could lose everything because of my "foolish" decision. I was prepared for that because I had spent the majority of my life putting everything on the line for the neighborhood with no returns. When you're doing that you have to develop a numbness to risk. Therefore, this was just another risk on my life I was just putting it out there on my terms unlike when I was in the streets risking it. Go all in and use the fact that who you could become is worth the risk of losing who you are at this particular point.

The Results

Insight

It was a long day in July as I awaited the decision from the twelve people who had the fate of my life juggling in their hands. It actually had been four days so far and the sleep difficulty was unbearable. I had lost five pounds and couldn't eat. Also, my girlfriend at the time had won her case and was no longer answering the phone and when she did I heard sounds of other men in the background before she would hang up. I felt alone, abandoned, and at my lowest point of being at that moment. The correctional officer's phone rang and he called me to the desk telling me to get ready because they had a decision. It's funny because I had been waiting for this moment however when it came my heart dropped and I was flooded with different emotions with the most prominent one being fear. Even right now as I write this my heart is pounding and my palms are getting sweaty.

Twenty minutes later everyone involved is in the courtroom and the lead juror comes out. I stared at this lady and plead with my eyes that she wouldn't be so harsh on me. I hoped that she understood that a kid's life was at risk from a mistake he made in foolishness. She looked at us and said, "On all counts of Assault in the first degree we cannot come to a conclusion and we are therefore hung." It wasn't a full innocence but it was close enough to alert the prosecutor that the next go-around we may win this case.

I was back in the unit overlooking my case ready to fight again when the unit phone rang. Another inmate yelled that it was for me and everyone who watched my fight for the last 14 months awaited impatiently. An older gentleman who had been supporting me said "That's your victory little brother. Right there on that phone, I promise." I smiled and headed over. In my head the entire battle was intended for me to get the prosecutor to budge on the twenty-five years he wouldn't come down from. I was willing to take 10 years at that moment. However, as God would have it I was informed that the prosecutor was willing to offer me 89 months in which I would only have to do 4 more years and go home. I agreed to the deal and when I hung up the phone a tear shed down my eye because things had come together since I had stood tall and fought my fight.

When I asked what made the jury unable to make a decision. I was told that I myself had convinced them that the Assaults in the first degree were sketchy and that no kid should go to prison for the rest of his life on a sketchy case. They were torn between maybe Assault in the second degree, which was a deal I ended up taken, that may have still given me 20 years with all of them together.

The fight was a hard one but I had won it. I decided who I needed to become, raised my expectations of myself, Jumped all in while still understanding that this whole thing was just a gamble. At the end of it all, that formula right there brought me to my success and is the only reason I'm able to be sitting on this comfy chair relaxing and wiggling my toes as a free man motivating you to Develop yourself into the individual you must become. Sometimes, you gotta do what you gotta do to bring forth your Success.

What will be your next Move?

What is it that you know must get done yet you are putting off?

Why are you putting it off (is it Fear, Lack of resources, Low expectations)?

Who must you become to achieve that?

<u>What expectations do you have for yourself in achieving it?</u>

<u>Are you ready to jump all in? When?</u>

<u>Have you accepted the fact that it's all a gamble and even if you lose you'll learn and fight back?</u>

<u>What would your results look like if successful?</u>

Jewel #2: Figure Out Who You're Not (DONE)

"I created a vision of David in my mind and simply carved off everything that was not David."

- Michelangelo

Two plead guilty, one acquitted in Tacoma drive-by shooting

By Kenny Ocker

kocker@thenewstribune.com

JULY 12, 2016 02:42 PM, UPDATED JULY 12, 2016 03:29 PM

Two men have pleaded guilty to lesser assault charges after a jury hung on counts of first-degree assault in connection with a 2015 drive-by shooting in Tacoma.

A companion was acquitted of aiding the men in the May 16, 2015, incident.

Omari Brown, 25, of Kent and Devonte' Parson, 23, of Federal Way were sentenced Friday in Pierce County Superior Court to serve nearly 7 1/2 years in prison, followed by 18 months of community custody.

It was September 2016, a year and some change since I had made my two-minute mistake at that bar that would now cost me five and a half years of my life. It's insane how we will sacrifice everything in the future to make due at the moment. It's because so many of us don't understand the concept between why we React and how to be Proactive. That lack of self-knowledge is what kills us in the long run. We tend to lose the battle of self-control to our emotions often and end up in bad positions.

Despite my effort to stay close to Seattle by putting in for a transfer to a prison that was near my home, I was sent all the way to the Eastside of Washington. For those who are unfamiliar with Washington it meant that the closest prison to my family was three and a half hours away, plus the eight-hour visit and three and a half hours back which, if you're hard at math, totaled a fifteen-hour day. Now, my kids' mom was driving out there with two kids in the backseat kicking, screaming, fighting, and doing whatever else crazy kids do. Therefore, it is by no surprise that there was usually dark energy already once the visits started because everyone was stressed. To top off the fact that I was far from everyone, they sent me to one of the most gang active prisons in Washington, 'Coyote Ridge Corrections Center.' Whenever I get to an institution since I'm a profiled gang member the special staff have to brief me for whatever reason. When I was doing my intake the gang staff says "Enjoy your homies you're going to love it here" and smiled as I left. I knew it would be a weird ride from there…Welcome to Coyote Ridge.

Hidden Jewel:

One thing that I hope you may have caught from my small account heading to prison is the Cause and

Effect. I really want you to harp in on the fact that a Two-minute dispute turned into Fourteen months of fighting my case (Stress, Depression, Anger, etc.), Loss of personal relationships and finances while fighting the case, Extreme stress on kids and their mother for years, and ultimately Five and a half years of my life. Not to mention the eighteen months I still had to serve under community supervision AFTER doing my time in prison. The high job offers, opportunities, intrinsic value of time spent with kids and family. I can go on and on about the losses I took from a two-minute dispute that could have easily been avoided by a simple "Let's leave this place has too much going on" or "My bad bro I didn't mean for it to come off that way."

There is a saying that goes "never make permanent decisions off of temporary emotions." I hold that true after the experience. Be aware of the choices you make in high-stress moments because that split second you have between thought and action could potentially save you from years and years of disaster in your life. Also, be conscious of the difference between Reactive and Proactive. The former deals with moving on a whim while the latter grants the moment of thought and clarity before moving forward in any direction. Proactive people are always going to win and reactive people can only lose.

Who Are You Not?

Insight

Now, I'm not going to lie and act as if I was just a saint throughout my incarceration on this journey to evolution. Anyone who has been living a certain way for 20+ years and one day decides to quit cold turkey professing that everything is all washed away and clean is a damn lie. Growth is gradual and requires all sorts of "sticking points" where it may feel like you will never overcome this one habit or shake these few people. However, if you are persistent and consistent it will happen and you will be far better than yesterday, but that perfection stuff isn't possible especially in a day. Strive for it and just make sure you're better than you were before then you'll be on to something.

I say that to let you know that I was foolish when I initially arrived at Coyote Ridge. Everything that I said in the county had damn near gone out the window at this point honestly. Mind you I was still sharp from the transformation due to having to study and wrestle with other sharp minds fighting my case. However, I still did foolish things. When I got in my unit the first thing I did was identify myself with the other homies from the Central District and G.D. letting them know I was there. Then, I was blessed with some weed to smoke, alcohol to drink, and synthetic weed to smoke for a different effect. I did everything with no remorse and when my homeboys felt some kind of way with another group I was right there with them feeling some type of way as well.

One day however I was asleep, high as a kite when I had an interesting dream. There was a lady correctional officer in my dream who was standing over me watching me sleep. I couldn't see her face but somehow I just knew she was female. While we lay there staring at each other I heard words come from who I believe was her and I'll never forget what she said. "De' Vonte' you're better than this. You have so much potential and if you'd just let it shine you could win the world." I woke up from that dream feeling refreshed and yet disappointed in myself. How did I just go toe to toe with the best and beat a life sentence but manage to have ended up here laying on this bunk high wasting my EARNED time? I didn't even smoke weed on the streets. What the hell was I doing? It was time for some deep reflection and change.

I remember being in this place of 'How do I begin this evolution' phase that I'm trying to do? I mean there are a lot of self-help books but I had never come across one that said: "Here, read this and you will change from who you are to who you want to be instant!" There were no young men my age who were trying to do the same thing nor had done the same thing. The older guys sort of stayed to themselves thinking all of the younger generations were too reckless to tie in with. So, there I was alone trying to figure out how the hell do I take the first steps in making this transition?

One day I'm reading Hill Harper's 'Letters to an incarcerated Brother' (which is an insightful book by the way) and the chapter starts with Michelangelo's quote "I created a vision of David in my mind and simply carved off everything that was not David." I thought "Wow, now if I could just get the vision of who I truly am I'll be able to shave off who I'm not." It took a lot of reflection but I figured it out and will share it with you all so that you can begin your transformations as well.

What Were You Told As a Youth?

Much of our future programming comes from what we were conditioned to believe about as a child as I stated earlier. Whenever you want to figure out why you think or move a certain way it is best to start your search where it all began in kid years. This way you will be able to pick up the good and take out the bad. Now, everything that is said about us when we're young isn't necessarily true. There are evil sadistic people out there who are just out to hurt you with the bullies in school who are lost. Those individuals mean nothing in your journey towards growth. However, there were truths told to us by people who really cared. Those things that enlightened us about ourselves were both agreeable and disagreeable. Those are the things we really want to look at to find our true selves.

When I was younger I would run around the neighborhood getting into all sorts of mess to the point parents didn't want me around their kids. I also had a difficult problem at school where a suspension occurred every week since first grade. However, the teachers and community leaders always used to say that I was a bright kid. They pronounced that whenever I got attention and would sit down to focus I excelled beyond my peers. They said I would be able to do great things if I learned how to harness my high energy and strengths. I heard that throughout my life but never let it stick because none of the "smart" kids would be my friends since I stayed in trouble.

Another point of reflection was when I remembered how I had always been good at reading and writing because my grandmother made me read books and look up words in the dictionary for myself. She would also teach me manners like saying "Thank you", opening the doors for women,

saying "ms. And Mr." and things like that.
Therefore, as I reflected more and more on these things I began to realize who De'Vonte' truly was at the core. He was intelligent, well mannered, and loved the attention from loving people. He wasn't the shooter, robber, and gang member society saw me as. Those things were only a persona I developed to survive in my environment.

Look back on what you were told that was good about yourself. Things that only the ones who truly knew you as a child would know. If nothing good was ever told to you then reflect on what good things you remember about yourself. Figure those things out first to give yourself a starting point. However, if you still can't identify anything good I want you to create them.

Then once you've done some reflecting on who you were as a child I want you to compare it to how you're living now. If it's not up to par with the good things you knew yourself to be at some point then it's time to make a change. Have you ever watched the movie 'The Curious Case of Benjamin Button?' It's a great movie in my opinion with many jewels about the power of living your life to the fullest while you still can. At one point in the movie his future daughter is reading the letters he had written to her as he was dying and he tells her "I hope you grow up to live the life you want and if you find out that you haven't, I hope you have the strength to start all over again." Even to this day, that quote makes me get a weird warm feeling in my heart. It is never too late to start over even if you're well into your life. As long as your heart is beating you have time to change your life and become the best you.

<u>Dig For Gold:</u>

I'm not going to let you just roll on past that one my friend. Really dig deep inside and pull out the treasure that you left buried from when you were young.

Ask yourself: What were some things people said about me as a kid that I could remember? What did I agree with that was negative? What were the positive things? Am I living those positive things out now? If not, what happened? Did I hold on to those negative things? If so, why and how do I let them go?

After you jot those answers down or save them in your mental Rolodex I want you to move on them. Here's a random thought. Why does it seem we can be told more positive things in our past than negative but allow the negative things to be held on to and speak louder than what's positive? We have to change that way of self-thought.

What Really Makes Me Feel Good?

Insight:

One day playing with my kids in the Coyote Ridge visiting room I noticed my daughter drawing on a piece of paper. Curious, I looked over to see what it was that she was sketching out. She told me it was a picture of what she's going to look like when she gets older. She told me that sometimes she draws other things like her home, kids, etc. This made me respect her imagination at such a young age and her ability to be forward-thinking. What it also reminded me of was how as a child I had a strong imagination and instead of drawing, I loved writing stories, creating gadgets, reading, and imagining the future. However, at some point in the adaptation to the lifestyle which the streets encouraged I lost interest in all of those things. The neighborhood and survival in it required all of my attention now. I couldn't get caught imagining unless I wanted a real bullet in my fitted cap. I wasn't able to think forward beyond the day because who knew if I would even be here the next day. There was no time to write stories because I needed to be holding the block down from the opposition. I had abandoned everything that truly made me feel good to adhere to the culture of where I was living. The sad part is that I tricked myself into believing that these things now made me happy and the rest of the stuff was just kid shit that had no place in my life anymore. In effect, I lost myself and many things that truly made me happy and took on what would later haunt my life.

"It is one thing to lose the people you love. It is another thing to lose yourself. That is a greater loss" was spoken by Donna Goddard on the detriment of losing oneself to the world around us. Self brings the strength of character that if developed to the fullest extent is unshakeable in the most trying of times. Therefore, if there is no Self then there is no durability.

On the road to finding oneself again through peeling off who you're not let's go back into what types of things are used to make you happy as a youth. Some people enjoyed art, some classical music, others may have even loved going on some sort of nature walks. Whatever it is that used to give you that warm fuzzy feeling inside is a part of what gave you joy at some point. Oftentimes we get indoctrinated in responsibilities and these responsibilities extend anywhere from "holding the hood down" to taking care of kids and bills. We get so caught up in "real life" that we dismiss the things that make us feel good to put on our "grown-up" hats. When we do this we either live a less than joyous life because there is no good feeling in it any longer or we replace them with false joys that we pick up along the way like "drinking", "smoking", etc. Not saying that either is a horrible habit I'm just saying that at some point you dismissed what your true happiness was brought on by.

In prison, I got back into writing once I looked back and remembered when I was a kid writing helped me escape my environment momentarily because I could be whoever I wanted to be wherever I wanted to be at on that paper. When I picked up the pen again and started writing in that cell it was so fluid and gave me that escape I so desperately needed again.

Another thing I did was I got back to watching animals which always brought me peace as a child. The grace in their movements and wisdom in the lion's approach to hunting made me feel good for whatever reason. My grandma couldn't take me to the zoo enough as a kid especially when I got around some snakes. Watching the National Geographic Wild helped me get back to my place of peace seeing the animals while I was in that cell.

Again, go sit back, reflect, and remember what brought you the most joy when you were younger. Once you begin piecing this together and add it up you will start making up your true self. There may have been some things you picked up along the way that you just filled the gaps with and don't bring you true joy just filling. Replace those with the truths were talking about here and you'll be on your path to where you need to be.

Dig For Gold:

Look back on your life and examine some of the things that made you smile. What were those things? Write them down and see which ones you can still do or are willing to pick up again when you create time to do so. Get back in touch with your joy and add that positive flow back into your life that's been soaked up by responsibility.

The Results

Remember that from the beginning the goal was to figure out who you were by digging deep into the past effectively to see who you are.

If you've followed the steps by reflecting on what you're doing right now that feels like it's not really you, remembering what you were told as a child, and bringing back what truly brings you joy, there should be a blank page left. This blank page is your platform to now create what you want it to look like on top of it. Through bringing out your authentic self and dispelling whatever is synthetic or what was just accepted your clean sheet should be staring back at you. Nicole Sobon said, "Sometimes the hardest parting isn't letting go but rather learning to start over." We must let go of the things that are gluing us to the false image of ourselves the world adheres us to and embrace the most difficult part which is starting over from scratch. I hope you have taken this jewel extremely seriously because it will be the baseline for your evolution and ultimately your manifestation into your truest form.

What's Your Next Move?

What are some things you may be doing now that are just fillers to what you're really missing in life?

How do you plan to get rid of those things?

What were some things that people told you about yourself as a child that were negative? Did you agree to these things and why?

What were some of the things people told you that was positive about yourself as a child? Did you agree to these things and why?

What are some of the things that brought you joy when you were young?

Are you still doing those things? If not, why did you stop?

Are you willing to pick them back up?

What's your next move to incorporate Jewel #2 into your life?

Jewel #3: Who Do You Want To Become?

"The only way it gets better for you is when you get better. Better is not something you wish, it's something you become."

- Jim Rohn

At this point in the journey, I had done what I had to do to get done what needed to get done and found out who I truly was by figuring out who I wasn't. That left me with one thing, It was time for me to decide who I wanted to Become. This was not an easy task because there were so many individuals in the world who had better lives than I did or who lived lives I aspired to live. Our instinct is to either shoot real high and not believe we can make it there or to shoot real low because we don't know what is possible for us. Either choice is not the best because neither ensures your greatest results.

I once attended a network marketing meeting with some ambitious leaders in their industry. I felt like I was in "quote heaven" and the Motivation just didn't stop. Yeah okay, I know that that's what they are supposed to do to fatten the calf for the slaughter but I didn't care about that at the moment. I was hungry for knowledge and they had it. One beautiful lady that spoke said something that I'll never forget because it defined my life up until that point. It was: "You don't always know what you want until you know what you have. You don't always know what you have until you know what's available. You don't know what's available until the people around you pay it forward."

I look at some people's environments like this. Hold on, by the environment I mean your Association, the Place you're living, and your lifestyle because of it all. Some of our environments are like a closed-off section in a restaurant. You have a menu that the waiter has given you that only holds five options. Therefore, we continue to order from this one menu even though the food is unhealthy, undercooked, and downright nasty. However, what other options are there right? Wrong. If you were just to look a little beyond your section you'll see that this place you thought was only a small restaurant is actually a buffet and there are people all around you getting their fill. The only way to know that is if you're curious enough to look and two if someone graciously sees you eyeing beyond your table and comes to bring you over there and show you how to eat as well.

My life was the projects and poor neighborhoods of Seattle, Wa. I had little influence outside of that and the very few amounts of times I was blessed to see the buffet I didn't feel I belonged so I ignored it and went back to the table. My scope was limited to that menu and there was nothing more for me to have I believed which made it a bit difficult for me to see who I wanted to be.

Hidden Jewel:

Notice that I continuously say "Believed". I only use that word when it is something that could and should be changed in our minds. In things, I want to manifest I use the word "Know". I know that there is an extreme difference between Believing something and Knowing, especially when it's

*something you're trying to bring forth. That's for
another build, however.*

To my main point here I want to press the fact
on you that the environment you "plant" your roots
in will affect your growth in so many ways it's both
scary and exciting. Scary because if it's the wrong
environment you'll eventually be choked by the
weeds and won't grow because it isn't the proper
climate for you. However, it's exciting because if
you place yourself in the right environment you will
grow exponentially and you'll become like an oak
tree with no limitations.

I speak to kids, young adults, parents, my
team, clients, etc. etc. and I all give them one piece
of advice to change their entire world. I tell them
that if you don't listen to anything else I have to say
then listen to me when I say plant your root in the
right soil in the proper environment and all else will
come together. I tell you this that you can put this
book down right now and follow that advice and
you'll find great transformation and extreme
success.

If you feel like you're not growing get out of
that environment. Again, your environment is
Association, Relationships, Home, Work, etc. I want
to get into the "How-To's of these so bad but I must
save content for the next book. Just follow this
script: 1. Disassociate from Negative, Inactive, and
Energy sucking people. 2. Find any way possible to

leave a home or neighborhood that holds you back by the people that live there as well. 3. If you hate your job and it's truly killing your productivity find something else FAST. The sacrifice of staying may kill you. Again, if you want true change, change your environment.

Figure a Vision

Insight

I usually say that a dream is something you see in your sleep while a Vision you can see with your eyes open. I don't chase dreams I go after visions. That is only my philosophy and I do not denounce the alternative. Whatever gets you up and at it in the morning by all means get to it. Whatever you do, put something in your mind beyond you that you want to get to.

In prison, I was now laying with a blank sheet that needed to be defined by what I wrote on it in my next decisions. I began by closing my eyes and envisioning what I wanted to look like, smell like, and even what facial expression I would have ten to fifteen years from then. I pictured myself wearing a nice tailored suit with dreads in a ponytail staring outside a top executive suite smelling like some expensive cologne. I had not yet Identified what it was I had become in that Vision, however, I was a success.

After seeing that, I decided well if I want to be of that stature one day let me start reading up on people already living that status and hopefully find some who started where I did. As I read, I became more introspective, sharper and ultimately my perspective broadened. I then was able to begin piecing together what it was I wanted to become and ultimately my Vision. Once I had direction the rest was history.

"If you are working on something exciting that you care about, you don't have to be pushed. The vision pulls you" was a quote by Steve Jobs I have found to be true. There is a fire that burns inside of you once you have a Vision for your life. It engulfs your entire being and you can't rest until you've served some part of it that day by taking action steps to make it a reality. Even just waking up feels different because you know that it's for a purpose.

Proverbs 29:18 clearly states that "where there is no vision a people perish." That is because without Vision or a clear direction on where you're going you are like a tumbleweed ending up wherever the wind takes you which is usually on the highway in traffic. Men and women who lack vision are more often than not taken advantage of and used as pawns in someone else's vision for life. The thing is you don't know what someone else may have planned for you therefore I encourage you to plan for yourself.

The first step in creating a Vision for yourself is to get an idea of where you see yourself in the future. Ask yourself questions like How am I mentally? Physically? Financially? What am I wearing these days? What type of lifestyle am I leading? How am I making my income? All of these things play into your total Vision. As they materialize in your mind begin weaving together into one picture of your future self. No matter how far you put it out just put it out there and the timing will come together as well. Remember, the main goal is just having a Vision at this point.

Once you have that Vision for yourself I encourage you to meditate on it when you wake up and before you go to sleep. Whoever you want to be then, work on becoming now. Through meditating you will begin to embrace the mindset of your future self and therefore your actions, thoughts, and habits will begin to follow suit. The key is evolving into that person you want to become from whatever place you are in life right now. That's the point of having a Vision. It's to give you something to work towards every day filling up every second of your being. You won't know it until you have tried. Get a vision and start making progress in your life.

Interactive:

Stop what you're doing right now! Okay, okay if you're too enthralled by the book so far you can do it later as well. Whenever you do it I want you to go off somewhere alone, No Spouse, No Kids, No Social Media, and think about your vision. If you already have it cool just take time to make it even sharper. What do you smell like, how do you feel, what is making you happy? However, if you haven't built out that Vision for yourself yet start asking questions like What do I look like? Where am I at? What's going on in my life at this point? Dream Big! Build your castles in the air and lay the foundation under it. The purpose is just to get an idea of where you want to end up. As these things begin to reveal themselves to you then write them down so we have a starting space.

<u>Get Around Like Minds</u>

Insight:

Do you remember being young and having to hear "Birds of a feather flock together?" Do you remember how corny and cliché that sounded to you at the time and thinking that whoever told you that didn't know what they were talking about?

I can distinctly go back to the time in my head when my grandmother began noticing a change in my behavior. I was eleven and had just started hanging out tough in the neighborhood I would soon flag for. At this point, I wasn't bringing my friends to meet her anymore how I used to because, well I just didn't care to anymore since I was a man now right? I could look out for myself and judge my situations huh? Stupid boy. Anyways, she never met my friends but could see the changes in my behavior like the pants sagging, defiance to her word, staying out later, and sometimes I could tell she knew I was high but didn't know how to address it without hurting herself.

One night she brought me into her room and said exactly that cliché saying that we all have had to hear at one point or another. "De' Vonte', birds of a feather flock together, and where they go you're gonna end up if you're not careful." That was all she told me and I walked out of her room without a care in the world.

The crazy thing about it is that that entire group I hung out with ended up doing time in prison. Some are dead now and others are just going back and forth through the system. Grandma ain't never lied and sitting in that lonely, dark, cold cell I was set to reflect on that.

I once read in 'Three Feet From Gold', a great self-help book on pursuing your purpose, that you are a combination of the books you read and the five people you spend the most time with. Looking back I hadn't read any books since a kid and I was EXACTLY like the people I had spent my most time with. Shoot, if you were different we didn't want you around preaching to us about being better it felt weird.

That reflection validated the truth for me. Now, what was I to do with it? At this point in my second year of being incarcerated, I had read many great books however I didn't know how to seek out like minds in the environment I was in. Then it dawned on me like Duuuuuuuuuuuuh! Like minds are going to be in like places therefore I just needed to put myself in the right places to be in a position to meet like minds. I wasn't too stupid after all huh, LOL. That encouraged me to enroll in school and begin taking whatever self-help classes the prison offered. Not only did I grow exponentially but I sure did find many other individuals who were on the same path as me.

Many of you right now are in a position where you want to change, yet you have not placed yourself in the best position to change. Your environment isn't conducive to the person you're trying to evolve into. I liken it to a palm tree being planted in Washington and told to naturally grow. Now if you've ever been to Washington you know there is not enough sun and too much rain to spark the growth of a palm tree. That is how a lot of our lives are. The friends we have surrounded ourselves with are negative, draining, or downright unhelpful to the cause. Then, the only things were reading are the latest dramas on social media, what's going on in celebrity life, or the craziness of "Fake News." All of those things are not shining enough sun and producing too much rain for growth. Note, sometimes it could even be an intimate relationship that causes the rain also.

The power of your association will change everything. Again, the power of association will change everything. The reason I say that is because once you've made up your mind and say that you are done with living below your greatness the next step is to figure out how to manifest your greatness. To do that you have to study and get around people who will bring that greatness out of you. I don't just mean passionate motivational speakers or seminar leaders. I mean individuals who just inspire you to be better by what they do on a daily that you can see. People where the fruits of their labor inspire you to plant your orchard. That is how an association will help build you. You will be around individuals who broaden your perspective, show you new places and give you a new light to grow under as you develop yours.

To get around those individuals you must first do the work yourself. How? Cut off going to any of the places that you used to frequent if the type of person you want to become isn't in that crowd of people. If they are then get out of your comfort zone and spark up a conversation with them on some universal topic like the economy or something. However, if not then find other spots via google if you have to where these individuals may hang.

Read books that challenge your way of thinking and cause great reflection. After that see if there are any book clubs where you can socialize in person or on the internet. Bounce ideas back and forth and maybe even schedule to meet up for further discussion.

You could also take classes and meet other students or even professors who are moving on the same frequencies as yourself. No matter what avenue you take to get hooked in with like-minded individuals, do it. Commit yourself to this growth in association and I can promise that if you're diligent in it you will soar to places you never figured before.

Keep Sharpening Your Mind

Insight:

You do not have to be religious to understand Proverbs 27:17 when it says "Iron sharpens iron, as man sharpens man." The like-minded individuals that you get around are there to help you get better as you are supposed to do for them. The sharpening should be reciprocated between both parties if things are to be fair.

As I began growing I ran into all sorts of individuals along the journey. Some sharpened me and would not allow sharpening from me because they felt that they knew it all. There were ones who thought that they weren't sharp enough to hold a conversation with me. Therefore they were intimidated by the very little knowledge I had and would come around every once in a while. Then there were the individuals who just wanted to be sharpened consistently and not show any results of the sharpening nor did they offer any sharpening for me themselves. The last type was the most draining.

I later decided that I would be an active student and make sure that I listened and learned attentively while at the same time I would also have something to give back to reciprocate the love. Therefore, I would be taking in energy yet also returning more energy as well. That is when I attracted more like-minded individuals to me and they enjoyed my company because I didn't drain them by only taking nor did I figure that I was the sole giver.

"You are a weapon stay sharp and seek balance" is a quote from Colin Wright. Staying sharp after being sharpened is key. Even the best of knives go dull after a while of use and if left for too long they will become useless until sharpened again. You never ignore your mind until the point of uselessness. You want to keep sharpening it and stay awake for the rest of your time on this earth.

What does it mean to stay sharp? Staying sharp in my personal opinion is to be continually stretching, growing, and renovating your mental capacity. It is to be on a higher level every month if not every day. You should not have the same limitations today as you had yesterday if you are staying sharp. This sharpness is intentional and doesn't just happen to you like that. You must pursue sharpness to keep growing.

I made that decision because the group of individuals I had begun surrounding myself with had the least knowledge which was perfect for me. However, I didn't want to keep sitting under their wings forever without bringing something back to the nest. Therefore, without their permission or guidance, I decided to seek ways to grow myself and boy did it work. They loved me even more now that I could offer some food for thought as well.

To stay sharp you just simply don't get comfortable with where you are currently in your growing journey. Continue reading, keep re-examining what you thought to believe was true at first, and share ideas to find others that challenge your thought. You want to always expand your way of thinking if you expect to remain sharp. Never get outdated unless you want to end up as Myspace did because of Facebook. Your new set of peers will love it too because now you're bringing in energy as well without just taking from it. Do this and you're definitely on the right track to Manifesting your Greatness.

The Results

After you have figured out your vision, getting around other like-minded individuals who have similar visions for themselves, and continued to sharpen your mind, things in your life should begin to change. You should be waking up with determination to be better and have more because you now have a vision for your life. This should give you a fresh feeling of excitement and fulfillment.

The new association that you have required should be bringing out the best in you. There may have been some pushback from you that could have sparked arguments however that's ok because its growth and none come without pain. Remember, this is new for you and uncomfortable. Accept the new sharpening and allow them to help you grow. Life at this point may be starting to look a bit different to you and that old belief system should be starting to crumble and allowing a new one to be built in its space. You're not stupid for rebuilding you're great for allowing yourself the freedom to start over.

Your mind should be expanding every day. At the end of the day and even sometimes in the middle of it, you should feel mentally exhausted. I once told one of my mentors that "I didn't know how mentally lazy I was until I started thinking." Your brain is a muscle as is your mind. Once you begin working out a muscle that hasn't been worked out before it is painful and extremely tiring. Therefore, understand that is normal and soon you will get used to that feeling but still be growing.

One last thing to warn you of is the comments you may get for being different. You may become the target of rash attacks on your character. Oftentimes it's from the people who you care about the most which will hurt the most. It's an okay warrior just suck it up and keep growing. One day, when you're surrounded in your glory it won't even matter.

What's Your Next Move?

Have you figured out who it is you want to become?

Write out what vision it is that you have for yourself.

How do you plan to start getting around like minds?

List some places that you will look into to find these individuals.

What books have you read recently?

How have they sharpened your mind?

-

Living It

Jewel #4: Be Consistent (2018)

"We become what we want to be by constantly being what we want to become each day".

- Richard G. Scott

Insight

There were times in prison that I hurt so bad because of the amount of loneliness I felt from having to isolate myself from what didn't nourish my mind. Individuals my age wasn't all too fond of a peer coming around "preaching" about doing better and being better even if he was from the neighborhood. I wasn't outcasted it's just I didn't fit in with the conversations anymore because of the level of thought I enjoyed discussing on.

I remember the last time I tried to get around a conversation that had nothing to do with the particular path I was now on. It was 2018 and I could potentially get out next year on an early release program that allowed you to do work release and house arrest on the streets for one year if approved. Up until this point my bid and journey of growth had been pretty much smooth sailing besides a skirmish or two and some heated debates. I made it to one of the best camps in Washington at the time, Cedar Creek Correctional Facilities. There were good dudes here and a lot of educational opportunities for me to pursue. Everything should be good from here, right? WRONG.

I was struggling with my identity as an evolved individual looking to motivate and evolve the masses. While at the same time doing my best to maintain my street persona to protect the reputation I had bled for. Over about a month period the camp had transferred a lot of individuals my age from the neighborhood whom I had grown up with and who had yet to meet the person I had become. Thankfully, they didn't knock it, it was more of a 'whatever' type of thing.

Well, over the days I had noticed some distancing between myself and the group. I then began hearing rumors that they were upset I had befriended someone from the opposing gang and felt it weird. One particular night I went over to where the guys from my neighborhood were and hoped I could just fit back in with them like old times. They were grouped up around the dayroom table (a common hangout area in prison) talking and when I walked in all conversation ceased. I came over and stood there with them looking stupid for a second all the while realizing they were uncomfortable to discuss in front of me whatever it was they were just talking about. I stood there for about five minutes hurting deep down inside because of the rift I felt between myself and the ones I grew up with and at one point would have died for. The distance was palpable. We shook hands and I left teetering between rage, sadness, and feeling like a burden had been lifted off of my shoulders.

When I walked out of that dayroom that night I knew that it was also time to walk out of the belief that I could balance two lifestyles at once. I had to either go all-in in my transformation or all in with my old party. I decided on the former option and sucked it up vowing to never try and involve myself in a situation that isn't conducive to my growth again. My consistency level rose another notch and the rest was history.

You, Will, Feel Lonely

-

As you transcend into this new form of being it is important to know that there will be times where you feel all alone in your world especially if you're starting this journey young. That feeling of being isolated is usually the beginning stages of evolution because you have not yet formed solid associations with like minds as of yet. However, don't worry, some of the greatest leaders who had the most impact on the world had to go off alone to grow. Jesus had instances where he went and prayed alone, Mahatma Gandhi left to meditate and Malcolm X went on his pilgrimage.

Robin Williams once said "I used to think the worst thing in life was ending up all alone. It's not.

The worst thing in life is ending up with people who make you feel all alone." When you get fed up with your old lifestyle the friends you once had and relationships you believed were key to your being become an irritant. You feel yourself feeling drained when you walk away from a group chat or telephone call with those individuals. There is usually some sort of distance growing between you that you can't explain. Eventually, you just become downright disgusted and end up feeling like that group no longer fits you. You just end up feeling alone even with them surrounding you.

Therefore, it is better to be all alone with yourself, having the understanding that this is not only temporary but also necessary for your Growth. When it's all said and done you will be able to rise out of the ashes and soar with other phoenixes of your nature. You will walk away from a group chat or a phone call feeling uplifted and ambitious about things to come. Those are the types of relationships you want anyway. The ones that nourish your heart, body, and soul while also enriching your mind.

Another person to be wary about even more so than your friends is your intimate partner. The one laying next to you at night or has connections to the deepest part of your being could be dangerous. If they don't share your ambition to be better and live a more positive, uplifting life he or she could be your downfall. We tend to overlook that because of our fear of being lonely as well. This fear is more palpable than losing our friends usually because we could deal with Tom and Linda leaving our lives since friends come and go. However, the one you love and claim not to be able to live without, no way it's not worth the pain. Yet let me tell you something. Jim Rohn said that "everyone has to make choices between two things, either the pain of Discipline or the Pain of Regret". The catch is once you forgo discipline you must endure regret which is a painful long-reaching scar. You don't leave that individual alone now because they're toxic, then once you realize it later the compounding effect of endured regret will eat at you like nothing else.

Another thing that usually causes us to fear being lonely is that we are not comfortable with ourselves. I know I had that going on for a while. I'm naturally an extrovert that likes to have people around me a lot to feed off of their energy. At this point, it's a choice and I don't necessarily need people around I just enjoy being around other people in joy. However, before I evolved to the point that I'm currently at I NEEDED people's energies around because I didn't like myself. You get yourself in a room alone and all sorts of things begin floating through your mind and if you're not happy with where you are at in life it will be a lot of things that you really don't want going around in your mind causing much discomfort.

The key is not to run away from these demons of thought but to embrace them, understand them, and change them. I had to deal with all sorts of demons in my mind when sitting in those cells. Initially, I tried to ignore, push away, or downright distract myself from having to hear them. Then I saw Dr. Strange...What you thought I was going to give you another quote from some globally known philosopher? I study life around me and gain understanding from everything, even superheroes LOL. In Doctor Strange the lady that's teaching him his powers tells him "You never defeat your demons, you just learn to live above them." That was extremely powerful for me. I didn't have to beat them outright, the thoughts were normal to have. I just had to gain an understanding of them and learn to be better to live above them. Therefore, if you experience those demons in your isolation stage just watch Dr. Strange......or you can listen to me and embrace what has you so uncomfortable and take back control.

All that being said I want you to expect a trial of loneliness and whatever has you afraid of it, make sure you defeat that and move forward.

Hidden Jewel:

Being alone, in my opinion, is one of the biggest fears of us as humans. That feeling of no security, love, or someone just to care at the end of the night when we lay our head on that pillow. The worse thing for many of us is the feeling of not being wanted. The thing is out of reaction we often subject ourselves to less than ideal living situations to be able to feel like "Somebody" cares for us. Think about friends you may have kept around only because you wanted to have someone to hang with even if you didn't feel comfortable with the activities. How about the groups you've inserted yourself into just to fit in to feel that sense of security. Also, the relationships that died long ago yet were held onto and probably still are being held onto because even if it's bad at least they're there with you. We've all done these things in some form of another and the effects have been far worse for hanging on too long.

I encourage you to take a second, all by yourself, to analyze who you've been dedicating your precious time to. Really dig deep and see if they are conducive to where you should be in life and where you want to go. Make a list of these people if you have to and compare your Morals & Values. Do their values match up with yours? How about their principles? I'm a firm believer in matching up each other's core morals, values, and principles to decide a friendship or relationship. That's important because if you guys don't run on the same gas when a situation occurs and you have to refuel there's going to be an issue. If you have yet to list your core fundamentals do so NOW because you're an even more dangerous space because nothing is directing your decision making. Check these things out and make adjustments for a more fruitful life.

The Tests Will Make You Best

Insight:

Living out the principles and values I've learned to develop into the individual I am today has come with tests at every angle. It's like as soon as you rise to be better you attract better people however you will also attract the opposing forces who are there to test your stance. If you fall short and stay down you lose but if you get hit and rise you're better than before it's as simple as that.

The tests that used to bother me the most were from individuals who were usually younger and didn't know the person I used to be. Due to their lack of knowledge on my history in the streets the respect level they brought wasn't necessarily up to my standards. I remember one younger individual, who was from a part of King County that was once considered a suburb and frowned upon to even have a gang there, decided he wanted to question my authenticity as a street reputable. First, let me say that I was out of pocket for grouping with young cats knowing my intentions weren't to build with them, but just to fit in for a moment and feel young and reckless again for a second.

We're all talking about the streets and the boy asks me with a disgusted look on his face "What are you even in here for?" Now, my initial response, assuming he figured I was some sort of pedophile or square that couldn't hold his own, was to check this kid and let him know who he was in the presence of. My blood was boiling and I looked at a couple of my homeboys from the neighborhood that knew me expecting them to say something to him. When they didn't I was even angrier. However, I had to take a moment to realize his ignorance of the situation. I had been that young man before and must understand where his mind is at. He felt that he had done some time and was tougher than most which are usual for young men in their teens and early twenties, especially a young black man in the gang culture. Therefore, I told him my story and what path I was on currently. I won't lie and say we became friends or that I even liked him afterward. What I will say is that instead of going down to his level I brought him towards mines and there was more respect born out of it. Tests are sure to come when you're changing, you just must be cognizant of them and work to the best of your Wisdom.

Tests arise to test the durability of what you believe in. When you claim a position you have to be ready to hold it down against the universe because it's coming swinging. Build up the mental fortitude to be able to stand your ground when these things come up against you. Also, you must look at them with satisfaction thinking "yes, I'm worthy of being tested for what I believe in." If you weren't then nothing would happen and you would go on living comfortably.

There is a quote that goes "Sometimes we're tested in life not to show our weaknesses, but to discover our strengths." When tests come our way we tend to get defensive and scared because the situation is uncomfortable. We want to back down in fear that we may not have been as ready as we figured we were. In prison, I would constantly doubt myself about what success I may or may not reach upon release. The tests were what I was scared of because if I proved not to be ready and failed then I believed it was all for nothing. These negative thoughts have to be let out of your mind. Yes, a test will illuminate your weaker tendencies or blind spots. However, the way you respond to them will help you discover strengths you never knew that you had.

When that younger individual tested me by questioning my authenticity as a person who came from the streets I was pissed, to say the least. When I withstood and overcame the situation I learned that I had more patience than I figured and that small victory gave me more confidence about my abilities when I went home. I knew that if I could practice patience so strongly in here where your reputation meant everything because you must be around these people every waking hour of your day; I could definitely do it in the outside world where you would probably never see someone who offends you again.

Therefore, use your tests as a catalyst to show you what you are truly made of. Come out on top of those tests stronger and better because of them. Gold has to go through the hottest fires to be refined into its purest form. The same thing goes for us. It may burn for a moment because you're not used to it but when it's said and done you will shine bright and have more value-added on to yourself because of it.

You Will Fail, But You Will Learn

Insight:

Every great task that you decide to undertake will not ensure success and great joy where confetti pops out of the sky, champagne corks are ready to be popped and people chant your names from rooftops. Shoot, that doesn't even happen to me when I do succeed.

The truth of the matter is that you will Fall, you will Fail, but you better Figure it out. When you fail, fail with a lesson in hand. Meaning, as soon as you realize that you have not brought forth your expectations in the situation start thinking about where things may have gone wrong, causing this outcome. Pull the lesson away from it so that you are a leg up for the next try. Yes, I said the next try.

I say that because you don't fail to quit, you fail to learn. Quick story about one of my failures in prison.

I was at the Coyote Ridge Camp at this point and there was a lot more room to run around freely here. An older brother and I decided that we wanted to bring some extra "money"(Food products that held monetary value in prison) into our situation. The heist would be to start a poker table and get paid off of every 'buy-in'. We executed perfectly and soon had a huge operation going. It wasn't long before there were disputes about who got 'Cashed Out' what when they won. People felt that some people were getting favored over others. The numbers were coming up short. Things were breeding madness and I was getting stressed. Despite my mentor's advice to "Leave it alone before you get yourself into something", I stayed greedy.

One day an older individual came into my room upset about the fact I told him he couldn't play at our poker table because he owed a debt to another race group that he wouldn't pay. He was talking to my roommate but using sarcastic remarks aimed towards myself. Me being the enlightened one and having practiced patience with wisdom should act in light of my teaching. I had been walking a higher path for two years at this point and now had individuals looking up to me. Guess what I did instead of using what I learned to diffuse the situation, I reacted out of emotion.

I called him some choice words and we fought right there in the cell. When it was all said and done I felt like a piece of stupidity. He got what he wanted and I lost a bit of confidence from the younger individuals who looked to me for wisdom. Truthfully, it felt like all I learned had really been for nothing because I had allowed an individual to outsmart me and get a negative reaction. However, my mentor pulled me up and said "Little brother, ante up and fail forward. Learn your lesson and keep pushing." I took his advice and for the next three years, I didn't fail IN THAT ARENA again.

Truthfully I don't even like to use the word failure when I'm building with individuals. I feel that nothing really is a failure. Things just didn't work how you expected them to and you have to find another angle. To me, failure means to have an ending. However, if there is another way to make it a success then how could it really be an ending? Every time things didn't work out how I wanted them, I was able to pick up a jewel from it and succeed in another way.

Thomas Edison once said "I have not failed. I have just found 10,000 ways that won't work. That statement there only adds to my perspective about the word and meaning of "Failure". There are three

points where Failure affects us in pursuit of any
goal:

The Beginning

I once read that "The biggest step that
requires the most faith and energy is the first one.
Anything after that is just tenacity." What they're
saying is that starting is the hardest part because if
you can start then you can definitely keep going on
to your victory. Failure usually attacks from the
beginning so we won't start. Have you ever been
about to take on some large task and in your mind
you hear things like "You can't do that", "This is
way too much for you", "What if things don't go as
planned and you don't have a backup plan?" Those
statements and many more have killed so many
dreams because they immobilized movement and
caused people to cease before starting. The fear of
Failure has overcome the Will to Succeed.

The Middle

'Tenacity' or being 'Tenacious' is simply
having the strength to keep going no matter the
circumstance. The thing about not giving up is it
clearly takes a lot of energy. When people begin
losing energy their thoughts go from "Yes, let's do
this" to "Can we still do this?" The reason is that
when you get tired you begin to justify reasons it
may be okay to stop right now. "I can't go on, I've
made it this far already, or Is this even worth it?"
Those statements are some of the things to be aware

of while you're running your marathon. Failure tricks you in the middle by making you believe that it's ok you have already gone far enough. Be aware because you're right at the tip of victory when this is happening.

The End

This point is when failure really has to work hard because you can see the finish line which boosts your will to keep going. I remember hearing Pastor T.D. Jakes preaches on getting everything you worked for but being so tired you can't enjoy it. Failure will now play on you from that angle. Small things will seem to jump in your path to upset you and challenge your perspective on things. You will be so tired that the finish line doesn't even look as appealing as it once did in your head. The fact that you made it this far and could just quit it all now really seems like a cool idea at this point because you're so tired. However, if you just keep going and turn your mind on mute right now you will succeed and everything that was said above will be invalid.

You see, failure or the fear of failure is like it's own entity that is extremely tricky. We think of it as a result but I believe it as a living spirit type thing that just feels your head with doubts and fears. Long before things don't work out how we planned them failure has already started planting seeds in our mind. That is why people break up in relationships long before they actually break up if you get what

I'm saying. Be aware of the fear of failure and learn to understand it so that you can overcome it. Once you establish this power of the mind you will be Unstoppable.

The Results

Living it and being consistent in living it has been one of the most difficult parts of this growth journey. I believe it's because you're in a constant fight with powers that are not of the physical plane. You're feeling lonely in the beginning because there aren't many like minds to associate with at this moment and your core group can't vibe. Then the tests are coming towards you to see how firmly you could truly stand your ground. You're all by yourself fighting an army with specific goals to bring you down. After all of that, you fail and are expected to learn from it after you've already been hit from a billion different angles.

However, once you overcome all of this I promise you will feel how it is all worth it. Not to be religious, but do you remember what Jesus had to go through to finally make it to heaven where he belonged. Then to top it off he did all of that to teach man that there were higher beings of themselves that they could become if they just tried. He was beaten, betrayed, looked down upon, isolated, and all sorts of other things to reach his highest form. You yourself are on the same path and just have to embrace the struggle to get there. Once things have cleared up I guarantee you will feel as tough as steel and as wise as a wizard on Harry Potter. LOL, I had to drop some humor in there for you.

What's Your Next Move?

Have you been consistent in your growth? In what ways has it been tested?

What will you do in times of loneliness?

What friends do you have who are in alignment with your growth journey?

Where can you go to make more friends who are on your same path?

Have you been tested on this path? How did you respond?

What did you learn from it?

In what ways do you see more tests coming?

Have you failed yet?

How do you plan to bounce back if you do?

Jewel #5 (Set Boundaries)

"Lack of Boundaries invites Lack of Respect."

Insight:

Before my incarceration, I was moving around whimsically throughout my life. To and From, Here and There not ever really getting anywhere. People were allowed long amounts of my time for no returns. Personal space was abused because I didn't care who I let around me as long as I had fun with them in some way. There were all types of crazy things I was okay with entering my mind not knowing the extreme damage it would do later.

What I didn't notice then was the disrespect my life was being treated with. My time was used and abused by my homeboys who would just hang around me and take, take, take then when there was nothing left they'd go somewhere else and take, leaving me empty. The types of women I kept around would just call me over for sex whenever they felt but didn't care to have me stick around after.

My house was broken into when I caught my case because I allowed multiple people, even some I didn't know from Adam, come over and party. Places in my apartment would be torn up the next day and trash would be all over the place with me left to clean it up. I even remember someone leaving a used condom in my bathroom after a long night of activities and expected me to clean it up.

With all of these people in my life of course the different philosophies of life came with them. Most, if not all, were extremely negative and downright ignorant. However, I didn't care because I was taking in whatever seeds were planted into my soil. Therefore, my moves were all over the place because I didn't have my own set of Standards and Values. The values I felt I had came from whoever was around me at any given time and which could change every week.

Now, that mess of a life I was living was horrible but it was a habit. Going to prison and learning to live by these new principles and set of values I developed were difficult but so much more promising. To protect my Time, Space, and Mind, all you really have in prison, I had to set boundaries and they worked like a charm.

Hidden Jewel:

Boundaries are extremely important to have set in your life no matter what walk you come from. People should not be able to just "pop up" in your breathing space without permission. We often ignore boundaries because we want to appear friendly, cool or it's someone close to us so we're obligated to let them do what they want in our lives. You are not obligated to anyone but your spouse and your kids.

Everyone else should ring the doorbell before they come in.

What begins to happen when you don't set boundaries is you get disrespected as a person. It's like a woman or man who's know to be really easy to sleep with. Although they may have many partners those partners treat them like a doormat that was given for free outside a garage sale. I'm just saying you must be extremely careful about how open your doors are in life because anybody may just walk in and some come to ruin.

Time

I once heard the rapper Kevin Gates say that "Time is the biggest loss because it's the only asset you can't get back." That pushed me to make sure that from then on out I would utilize my time wisely in prison and on the streets. Wealthy individuals look at their time like money because it truly is. Time is a currency that is traded consistently. You get to pick if someone is getting over on the trade or not by who you allow your time to be 'spent' with. It could be invested in an uplifting and informational conversation which would be a good stock or a draining one which would be bad stock.

The thing about time is it doesn't even have to be 'spent' with an individual to be wasted. You can waste your own time by thinking for no reason.

What I mean by "Thinking for no reason" is harping on things in your mind just to feel sad, bad, or with no purpose at all. Your thoughts should be focused on solutions and building your kingdom in the mind first. Thinking should never be allowed to just wander around aimlessly as if there is no purpose to having a mind to call your own.

I took heed to this lesson when I began having too many programs I was attending and not enough time to still sow into other individuals I was mentoring or for myself. I had to sit back and really establish what truly mattered when putting my vision into perspective. Once I did that a lot of things and people had to get cut off the chopping block and my energies became focused on what provided the best return.

How:

1. When it comes to people you may be friends with, learning from, or mentoring you must still prioritize your time. I like to go by the 80/20 rule that states you should focus on the 20% that gives you 80% of the results. In people, that would be a couple of friends who give you the most energy and feeling of kinship in life? When it comes to people you are learning from time goes to who sows the most seeds and speaks what's most conducive to your vision? When it's about who you may

be mentoring, who is showing you the most return? Who is the one or couple that has shown the best results for what you're planting in them?

2.   When we're discussing things that you're doing where is the most satisfaction coming from? In which classes are you actually learning the most? This doesn't mean you must cut them off and never pick them back up again. It just means for right now you're focused on what is the most important you'll be back for what's left later on.

<u>Space</u>

Your private time and personal space are extremely important, especially when you're constantly thinking about how to be a better version of yourself and building towards that. I think this is the most overlooked area in an individual's life when they are trying to figure out why things are so stressful at some point. If everyone is in your 'mix' and you are allowing anybody to just walk up and soak in your space then you're bound to pick up bad vibes and be left with a filthy house (speaking figuratively).

I remember an old convict who mentored me at a point in my incarceration that said "Little bro, everyone doesn't deserve to be in your six feet." He explained to me how you have a six-foot radius and anyone who you allow in it could and usually will change the energy levels around you for good or for bad. The key is to keep the bad out and only let the good in. It's extremely difficult to do, especially when you're not trying to appear rude, but it's worth it.

Elizabeth Awori once said "Protect your space. Let people earn the right to be in it." We too often give our space away for free just like we do our time. Both donations of precious luxuries stem from an unintentional life. When we know what we're our goals are that knowledge allows us to know what would be a waste of time. We can get a good idea of who would be a waste letting into our space. I often watch individuals for at least a week (via social media) before reaching out to them or allowing them to be accepted by me. It used to be from a prison practice, yet now it's a common thing for me. I study a person's mind by watching three things:

1.   What they talk about

2.   What they are doing in their pictures

3.   Who they are around or corresponding with

After I get my synopsis there you either pass or fail in my "you can come around me" files. Many are looked at, few are chosen. That is something you should live by as well when it comes to your personal space.

Mind

Mind, one of my favorite things to talk about when I'm discussing the ability to evolve. Yet, the mind is also the trickiest to discuss because there are so many levels and hidden capabilities of the mind that have yet to be unlocked. Then there are parts where some of the most learned individuals disagree on. However, everyone agrees on two things when it comes to your mind. One, the mind is real and Two, you have to guard what you let into it.

The prolific Motivational Speaker and Author Jim Rohn said to "Stand guard at the door of your mind." Meaning you must always be diligent in protecting what you're allowing to cross your mental threshold. Understand this can come in various forms. Friends can be talking about some things that are negative that plant seeds in your head. There could be a movie or television show that ignites bad energy within you. It could be something you read something you see. There are no limits to how junk can enter your mind.

I remember when I was inside we were finally blessed to get a new cable subscription and a channel came on that showed "Gangster – A – Thon". They played back to back real documentaries on thugs and gangsters alike. I watched that one day for four hours straight and didn't realize until I was sitting on my bunk later that I felt darkness within me for some reason. The feeling didn't feel good, yet familiar. Once I really reflected on what was going on I realized that I had been literally thinking about my neighborhood and evil activities I should have pushed a harder line in when doing them. Watching that series had me feeling like I needed to go out there and do more, even in my evolved state. Safe to say that that was the last time I binged on the gangster material.

What I am saying is that seeds can be planted into your mind without you even noticing it. If they are not discovered soon and pulled out of the ground then they will grow like weeds. The environment that will feed them are other subtle negative drops of information you pick up unintentionally throughout your day. The next thing you know is one morning you wake up and there's an entire weed stock-taking over your backyard. Again, Beware of Friends, Conversations, Social media posts, music, television, and anything else you set your mind in front of for any given amount of time. Guard your mind.

The Results:

It is extremely important to set solid boundaries in your life or no one will ever have respect for it. There are many areas where the caution tape may need to be put up however Time, Space and Mind are where I saw it was most effective in my life. If you find other areas in your life where you notice people intruding in and it's draining you then please put up your stop signs there as well.

Once you begin to erect these boundaries please understand that individuals will probably now see you as "Funny Style" or acting "Weird." That's okay. You'd rather be at peace with yourself than in chaos because you're not allowing respect for yourself. Once you have successfully put these boundaries in place and are practicing them you will experience almost a euphoric feeling of peace. Things in life will begin making more sense to you and your growth will increase exponentially. Love yourself and begin guarding what's yours.

What's Your Next Move

1. Have you ever set respectful boundaries before? Did people abide by them? If they didn't, how did that make you feel?

2. What are do you feel like you most need to set up a boundary in Time, Space, or Mind?

3. How do you plan to set this boundary? How will you continue to set boundaries?

4. What other areas in your life do you see a need for boundaries and why?

5. What's stopping you?

Jewel #6
"Seek to Understand, then to be Understood."

-   Stephen Covey (7 Habits of Highly Effective People)

In our culture, it is common for us to try and get our point across without waiting or even wanting to take in what the other person is saying. It can turn into a type of verbal arm-wrestling match where each individual is attempting to oppose their will on the other.

It is especially easy to just block out what someone has to say to get yours out when you believe you're smarter or have more experience in what you're talking about. You already have in your head "He or she doesn't even know what they're talking about. Who are they to talk over me?" Trust me I have been that guy a time or two especially when I grew wiser. In those times I thought that if you didn't read as many books as me, take as many classes, or help transition as many lives you had no right to speak. That was a horrible mentality.

As I acted like a high-nosed buffoon the same people I was trying to reach began staying away from me. The individuals who did want change and admired my "walk" would not dare tell me or even come around me. Old friends who knew me from the neighborhood who had now begun respecting the evolution said that "I acted like I was better or smarter than everyone." The weird thing is as "awakened" as I thought I was I didn't even see what was going on. I do believe that we can have our heads so far up our own butts that we don't notice the poop all on our faces.

I had to run into an older individual who was far more enlightened than me to see the problem in myself. This aged gentleman was one of the wisest people I had met yet he still did not realize his one flaw. He would teach, teach, teach to you without listening to you at all. If you disagree with something he said, even if there were a valid reason, he shunned you and would rant on how he was right. When I noticed that I noticed I had to change. First, let me explain the build-up to this realization.

Make Relations

My thought process around 2018 – 19 was that I could teach everyone and knew everything although I didn't notice it at the time. I also figured that anyone who asked questions wanted to be "taught" and therefore had to become my "Student." Going around taking a bunch of guys "Under my wing" made me feel needed and important in the community I was in. There was no need to discuss anything outside of what I was teaching you because what I said was all that mattered. A fool I was, a true fool I was.

That selfish approach probably caused me to lose more people who actually needed some guidance than I will ever know. I began wondering why certain individuals who once admired me were pushing away and becoming more distant than usual. They started hanging around other intellectuals my age and older, learning from them and spending time. In my ignorance, it looked like they just found new playmates in these individuals and nothing would come from it. Therefore, I shrugged my shoulders and kept it pushing.

The thing about success is it requires no explanations when the results are right in your face. I began watching these young boys transform into young men whom I myself was attempting to groom them into before. The only problem is that they wouldn't receive it from me how they were from the other men my age obviously. This hit my ego and I would love to tell you I learned from it immediately but I didn't. I continued to believe it was the people I chose and not me. That it was their loss and I just wasn't the right "teacher" for them. Packing my ego up I walked away from them and their journeys not even caring to compliment them on their growth.

It wasn't until months later when I read Stephen Covey's "Principle-Centered Leadership" that I gained an understanding of what the issue was. He says that three things must happen before you can gain permission to lead someone. He said you must first model what it is they want to become. Second, you must gain a sincere relationship with an individual. Lastly, you ask permission to teach. I would blast past relating, skip permission, and just start teaching. That approach pushed a lot of people away from me. Once I read that text I started back from the beginning and lived out my demonstration. When the individuals that had walked away began talking to me here and there I would ask them how they were doing sincerely and really care. I asked about their families and what were some things they had learned recently. The funny thing is the more that I did this the more I actually cared for them with my heart. Things went from a "Teach" relationship to an actual friendship. Before I knew it they were back around with many more young adults. Being around them was more fulfilling for me because it was like spending time with friends who just happened to really want to know what it was you were doing. That taught me that making relations before anything else is important when building with someone.

Hidden Jewel:

I find this to be incredibly important when building any type of relationship in general. If you want a true authentic involvement with anyone you must go further than skin deep. The questions should be more than "How are you feeling?" then you accept a "Good" and leave it there. Really ask them "What made you feel so good today?" with a genuine smile on your face.

Do this with every individual you encounter and you will see how your relational IQ grows exponentially and people will seem to flock to you. This isn't a manipulative tactic if you're truly sincere, which will grow on you, in wanting to know more about the individuals.

Meet People on Their Levels

Insight:

I once read in a book that "Consciousness" is 'Knowing why people are where they are and understanding why you're not where you could be.' Take a minute and digest that because it could be read in a few different ways. This statement could not have come at a better time for me because this was at that point where I was being real arrogant thinking that I was to teach everyone without listening or getting to know them.

Another bad habit I had happened to pick up was looking at individuals and judging them by the levels they were currently on. Even saying that sounds bad smh. When an individual still at the beginning phase in their journey made a mistake I would come down on them hard and compare my own discipline to their lack of it. When we had conversations I would speak condescendingly as if I was high almighty and they should know better. Again, this caused me to lose a lot of people and had some apprehensive about letting me know their struggles.

Once I read that statement on consciousness, what I considered I was, I had to raise my levels of awareness. Taking the time to understand why they were at the level they were on, because I had been there once as well, allowed me to gain a better understanding and relate more profoundly. The conversations turned more into "How can We move forward?" rather than "Why are You doing that?"

Once I had a good understanding of their level I was able to see how I made it through those levels and used my routes as assistance rather than chastisement. I also was humbled because I realized

I wasn't even at as high a level as I thought I was and had to gain an understanding of why I wasn't there yet. All in all, I was humbled by the statement which allowed me to grow closer to people who wanted to build with me and also helped me to grow my level of Understanding.

One of the key ingredients when learning to understand an individual is learning to fully understand their situation and why they are in it. I don't advise offering any sort of prescription to a perceived problem without first knowing thoroughly what the cause is. When you go to the doctor you're examined than prescribed. Vice versa could cause you serious damage as will trying to prescribe a solution to a problem that is not understood.

Living out your new being gets tricky because more is expected of you now. There are a lot of people who will be hoping to learn from you but also just looking into what you're doing and wanting to sabotage it. You must be able to understand both approaches and deal with them accordingly. Even those who seem to be negative and you may not even feel like helping are deserving of seed and you're the planter. Taking on a journey of growth also bestows you with the responsibility of planting seeds in every land you come across despite how much you may not enjoy the place.

Now, when I say to "Meet people on their levels" I don't mean dropping your morale or principles to sow a seed. I do mean you may have to come off your high horse to speak with a stubborn drug addict, young gang member, or even just an arrogant asshole about life. Though initially, you may hate every minute of it the fulfillment you will receive from doing it is exuberating.

This also doesn't mean that you must spend every waking hour sowing seeds into individuals that may not want to grow at that moment. Doing that will be frustrating and could eventually deplete you of your energy. Continuously attempting to sow seeds into someone who doesn't receive it, to me is like throwing a hundred punches at an opponent and missing everyone. Anyone with basic boxing knowledge understands that a missed punch takes away more energy than a connected one. Sow your seed and allow the higher powers to do the due diligence.

All in all, just be sure that you allow yourself to be humble enough to speak with others at the level they are at in their journey if they aren't as far as you. No real champion of life will ridicule the beginner. A true champion will give you tips to make it to the championships. Remember, though you haven't won everything you are the champion because you've championed different levels in this life. However, don't forget to reach back and help others as well.

Accept People as They Are

One of the best programs I got myself involved in was Toastmasters. Besides the great communication skills, leadership qualities, proper verbiage, and many other great things, Toastmasters taught me how to socialize with and accept people as they came. This was actually taught to me in three phases as I accepted different leadership roles within the program. I will breakdown those phases as we get further into this chapter.

Toastmasters in the "Free world", in my opinion, has a totally different reputation than the one in prison does. Out in modern-day society, the program is looked at as an honor to be a part of and a great educational tool utilized in businesses around the globe. However, despite what the blind and deaf will say, in the prison community, a majority of the population believes that Toastmasters is a haven for social outcasts or those who would be considered "weirdos" amongst the prison culture. Being a part of the group especially heavily involved could get some real boo-boo thrown your way if you don't hold a solid position amongst the community.

Initially, I fell into the guise of believing the hype. Honestly, it wasn't words or rumors that led me to see it as a weird place. The rumors may have sparked a bias in my mind but I tried it anyway. My first experience was okay until I came back a couple of more times and saw some really weird things going on that I won't go into here. However, that was at a medium facility that usually has a lot of weird stuff going on regardless, if I'm just being honest. Therefore, I left it alone until I got to camp at Cedar Creek Correctional Facility and was invited. Again, there were things there that were awkward for me. However, the core group was pretty solid and kept me participating. There was a lot of ridicule from people I had known already for years and some actually hurt, yet as I grew in position there I grew to learn people and understand them. Once I took that approach things didn't matter because I knew that the people who talked stuff didn't have the understanding I did therefore were not able to see what I saw in that club. I credit that place with granting me the ability to really "Get" people no matter their character and accept them as they were.

Secretary: Taught me to observe and record people's positions.

The first leadership role I took in Toastmasters required me to jot everything down said in essential meetings. Being a secretary is actually a busy job because you must be accurate and on point with what's being said or the whole system may collapse. I was joking but it is a serious position. When any power move within the organization has to be addressed from the past all fault falls on the secretary.

Having this responsibility taught me to keep my ear sharp and pick out the nonessential information from what was really important. However, what it also taught me was to gauge a person's agenda. By seeing what people voted for, vetoed and the politics behind the scenes I learned to know what they held away from the people who sat before them. In essence, I learned their truths and how to accept them rather I agreed or not.

Vice President of Education: Taught me to ask questions and find the WHY.

The next position I took on was after about six months into the program. The Vice President of Education is probably the most interactive of all of the positions because you must assess a person's skill level and work on a plan with them to reach their educational goals. As a secretary, I sat back and listened while just recording what I heard. Now I had to get in the mix with every individual and learn about why they attended and where they expected Toastmasters to take them.

As I look back, this position may have caused the most effective growth within me because it allowed me to see the good that was in everyone. Sometimes it is extremely tough to do that. Yet, to truly be an agent of help you must learn how. The reason why I could see the good was that pass the mean exterior, disagreeable charge, unkept hygiene, etc. etc. I was able to learn what their true ambitions were. Myself being a man of ambition, I hold a bias for those who want to make big things happen themselves. Therefore, as I went around figuring out goals for them, placing them on the right learning path, and following up on progress I got to know the person and not the image. After discovering those hidden gems all of the extras that were thrown on top of them really didn't matter to me. Seek the good in individuals and it'll be a lot easier to accept what you perceive as negative.

President: Taught me to lead different background types and communicate in various ways.

You would think that becoming the president of any organization is the best position because you are the "boss" and can make decisions for all. The thing is the president, at least an effective one, is the largest servant of the entire team. When I had taken on this role within the club I had to always be available rather I was irritated, sad, lonely, or just wanted to be left alone. This was actually my goal when I began Toastmasters however it wasn't as easy as I figured it would be once I got it.

Wow, this being my ultimate goal and ironically the last role I played before being released from prison I learned so much. However, for the sake of focus, I will only speak on how it also taught me to accept people for who they were. Leading a team of various personalities, backgrounds and agendas were extremely tough for me starting. I always used a blanket approach to "dealing" with people and if you didn't accept it you were out. However, as the president, I could no longer do that and had to tailor my approaches to the individuals.

This means that after I had finished my term as Vice President of Education, where I had to thoroughly assess the participants, I was pushed into a position where I had to fully understand my team. Dealing with people who are learning and dealing with people who are teaching with "power" I found out are two different things. Those who are looking for our help to be educated oftentimes were more humble because they understood that they didn't have enough understanding of the things being taught in the program to argue or change anything just yet. However, the team who were teaching those that were learning felt as if they had it all figured out already. Each individual brought their own agendas to their positions of power with their own twist in doing things.

Therefore, what I did was sit down with each member of the team and just get to know them. I found out why they chose leadership roles within the club, what was their history in the club if they came from others and who they were personally. We would eat together in units, talk about books, say hi to each other's families in the visit rooms, and just build together. This allowed me to really get to know them and I won't lie as if each member was agreeable to me because they weren't. What they were was my team and therefore I had to accept them as they came. What they were willing to work on changing we did and what they weren't we left alone.

Of all this, if you notice one thing is it's all about getting an understanding of who you are engaging with. Once you have an understanding, rather you like them now or not, you will see that you most likely won't change them without consent. This leaves you with two choices, leave or stay. However, there are circumstances in life such as Work, Family, Clubs, etc. that you can't just leave. Those circumstances are when you must accept a person for who they are and understand why they are like that. This doesn't mean you have to be best friends it only means you must accept it and move on. Understanding is key in any progress especially when it comes to people.

The Results:

There's a saying that goes "You can't judge someone until you have a full understanding of what made them who they are today." I know that statement to be true and expounding on that, once you have a full understanding you won't want to judge them anyway. If anything you would want to help or feel empathetic towards their situation.

In this point of "Living It" I learned a lot about myself from the mirrors of others. That means that some of my best growth in this part of my journey actually came from what people showed me about myself and I bounced off of that. Once you are humble enough to make relationships with people regardless of what stage in growth they are on you will see the difference it makes. Then when you choose to mentally meet them on their levels the bond will thicken. After that, you will truly have a sincere heart for that person and will be able to teach and/or just relate.

When it is all said and done, at this point you should be an example for the world yet a student of life. Books will still be your go-to but life will be your everyday study. The people who come into your life will appreciate your humility and favor being around you because you care. Once you've reached this point there's nothing left but Being.

What's Your Next Move?

1.   What does 'Having an Understanding' mean to you?

2.   When was the last time you intentionally formed a relationship

with someone just to fully understand their situation?

3.   **What will you do next?**

BEING

Jewel #7 (Be Humble)/2019

"Humility will open more doors than arrogance ever will."

\-   Zig Ziglar

    We have come to the part of our journey where the greatest opponent has now become one's self. You vs. You is what I like to say. Earlier in our coming of age, we allowed circumstances, people, and situations to dictate our moves out of reaction. Although we grew from those mistakes, we understand at this point that the key is to be proactive. Everyone is a mirror of ourselves and can help us continue to improve and increase our productivity in life.

The word "Being" in the dictionary means 'The nature or essence of a person'. What I mean by titling this section Being is to point out that you traveled through the journey of becoming who you wanted to, Living out the principles of who you had to become and it is finally a part of your Being. It's natural for you to be Understanding. It's regular for you to be consistent with who you truly are. You don't have to search for you because you know You. That is Being. However, some challenges come with Being as with anything else. These challenges are from within and could be difficult to combat because succumbing to them is easily justified.

In this section, we will address some of the things that could cause us to fall short in our newly acquired levels. I want you to be fully aware of where the traps are and how to avoid and/or overcome them. Please join me in this final section of our journey as we Grow and Develop our Beings.

Point Out Greatness in Others First

Insight:

One of the many flaws I noticed about myself during this time is that I was extremely arrogant. Initially, I figured I was a humble dude from very humble beginnings and therefore quiet about what little I did have. However, upon reflection, well actually after pointing the finger at a bunch of people I thought were arrogant irritants, I decided to look deep within at my own ways of being.

An older man who had been incarcerated for about ten years enlightened me when he said "People are just a reflection of yourself." I didn't agree right away until I noticed that the same individuals I found myself not liking, if I looked at why I didn't like them, it was usually because of a flaw within myself. It just so happened that I hated arrogant, boisterous, cocky dudes that thought they were the world. Well, using the mirror tactic I found some not so good things that were similar inside of myself.

My arrogant ways were hidden under how I treated people who I felt were "less than" myself. The cockiness was shielded with small jokes about how I look better or am more fit than an individual. My boisterous behavior came out when I was whooping someone in a game and screaming out how weak they were and how nice I was. Those traits were the exact traits that I extremely disliked in everyone else. That realization humbled me. Knowing that there was somebody or some people that had been watching me be this arrogant butt and held me with disdain as I did the others made me want to change.

I doubled down and thought to myself 'What can I do right now to increase my humility.' Noticing that when you sincerely brag or compliment another person first you take your own eyes off of yourself I knew that that was a great starting point. My mind was made up that from now on in any interaction I was going to find whatever good trait in an individual I could and by complimenting them I will give them the floor. When I began this practice great things started to happen.

One of the greatest tools in communication is to compliment someone. It is something that works at any point in a conversation as well. In an ice breaker you can say "Hey, that shirt really looks good on you." In the middle of a conversation the only time you can get away with cutting someone off is by stopping them mid-sentence and saying "Wow, you really have a great set of whites." The most effective, in my opinion, is at the conclusion when you would say "Before you leave I must let you know that whatever scent you're wearing is exceptional." Either of those well-placed comments will leave the person you're communicating with in butterflies.

The art of giving a compliment before boasting about yourself actually helps sharpen your being in a few different ways.

1.   You're finding the good in an individual you may not fully agree with or even like

initially. By finding the good in even them you are breaking past the surface and giving them a chance to be seen in a new light by you. Thus, starting a potential new relationship.

2.　The person you are communicating with now sees you as a selfless individual and may be more willing to engage with you on various levels. Truthfully, you're training yourself to become more selfless and caring by doing this.

3.　Humility is building inside of you because your mind is being conditioned to look for greatness in others and ignore your own ego which is an honorable gift to have.

The thing is you must be sincere when giving these compliments to people you are engaged with because for starters it isn't honorable to lie to someone about what you think of them. Also, people can tell when you're not being authentic. Being untruthful will put them off and potentially ruin your image and credibility as a wise individual. Although that may not seem too bad we have to realize that each person we interact with is only a few people away from the person who can help us get to the next level, if it isn't THEM.

Therefore, search out and bring to light the greatness in others before complimenting yourself. That will breed some of the best characteristics one can have in self. You will also find that more people will be attracted to you and many more doors will open in your favor.

Look, Listen, and Learn

Insight:

I once told an O.G. in prison who played a part in mentoring me that "I didn't know how mentally lazy I was until I started to think." He loved and complimented me on how profound that statement was. My intentions weren't to sound wise at all. I felt like I had just spent my first week working out and now felt the pain so badly that the comment was generated half expressing how I wanted to stop. However, it came off as wise which was fine with me.

My life up until this point could have been compared to an empty paper bag blowing carelessly in the wind. There was no rhyme or rhythm to it, very little direction and it seemed the only pattern was I kept ending up in somebody's handcuffs. I gave little energy to thought unless it was the basic instincts I needed to survive and since it was instinctual, habits instilled in me from the neighborhood to "make it", there wasn't really any effort of thought expended.

Therefore, when I was in prison and started to study life around me, my mind felt overwhelmed by the end of the day. What I was doing as a student was taking notes, evaluating those notes, and thinking on them until I gained a full understanding of the subject. This was a lot going on for a young dude who didn't even think past "make sure that the car coming down the street was a familiar one and not the opposition."

As I grew used to this new way of using my brain it became even more simple and I actually started to enjoy learning everything around me. It was like working out, you came knowing that it was going to be tough in the process, yet great in the end. To this day there are times where fatigue hits my mind because I'm learning at an entirely different level, but I know that soon this will become simple as well and I will grow just like I did in prison.

Hidden Jewel:

You could not read a book for the rest of your life, which I strongly advise against, yet study life and be great. When the world around me began to unfold as one big school my level of wisdom began growing so fast that I had to take quick mental breaks. That's because everything around you can literally be something to grow on and add to your arsenal of thought. If you haven't already, I advise you to begin studying every interaction between yourself as well as others. Watch people and how they move and think. Look up great philosophers and their thought. Study your kids if you have them and dissect the wisdom out of their moves. Just really learn from everything and your Understanding of life will flourish.

There's an adage I once heard that goes "There once was a wise owl on an oak. The more he saw the less he spoke. The less he spoke the more he heard. That's why we should all try and be like that bird." I won't lie and say that as soon as I heard that I listened. However, over time it became essential to my growth. Let's breakdown the importance of being able to LOOK, LISTEN, AND LEARN.

Look (Observe):

When I talk about "look" I mean to really "Perceive" something or "become conscious of" which is the true meaning of "Observe." To do this one must really register what they see before their eyes. Too often what is on the surface is taken as just that, what is on the surface. We see the people who make us "Feel" as good as great friends or even lovers. Those who make us "Feel" bad are enemies. However, we often don't take the time to dive deep into the causes of whatever vibes those individuals are sending our way. The "Good Feel" people may not be good for us if they only make us feel good when we're subjecting ourselves to living below our greatness to be around them. The "Bad Feel" people may actually be good for us if the only reason we don't like them is that we disagree with the fact they don't like how we're not living up to our full potential and are actually offering feedback geared towards building us up. That's why it's important to deeply perceive the things we take in for only face value.

The drawback for many of us is subconsciously we know how much mental energy it takes to truly look into something and thus avoid it. We only want to look into it if we know it will affect us immediately. We don't take the time to think that certain things will have long term effects if we don't properly dive into them. That also doesn't mean that they always have to be negative. I've let go of people that would have been better for me in life in the long run, but in the present, they were against the way I was living and I felt judged. Had I looked a bit more deeply into the relationship I may have been able to perceive the truth they brought to the table. However, it was squandered and I don't want you to do that. If you already have I don't want you to do it again. Therefore, seriously LOOK into a situation and find its deeper meaning at all times.

Listen (Not Hear):

Have you ever been in a conversation with someone and once it was over you barely remember any of the key things they were talking about? Have there been moments where you were in a heated debate and while the other person was speaking you were just formulating your response using tidbits of information you were able to catch? If so, you were not listening at all. You were hearing what they were saying without processing it.

Many people tend to perceive "Hearing" as "Listening" and are upset when the results are not what they expected. True listening skills come when an individual has the ability to hear what the person is saying and process the information to gain an understanding with an open mind. Then they'll formulate a response at the appropriate time. Often the best way to convey that you understand what the person has said is by paraphrasing back to who you're communicating to what you took from what they said. Listening in this productive manner is the only way you will be able to get authentic information worth great use.

However, there is another step to listening. There is an adage that goes "A wise man hears one word yet understands two." When I'm listening to an individual I'm gauging their Words, Body Language, Previous actions, etc. to get a full understanding of the message they are attempting to convey. In my opinion, you can't have an accurate reading of a person until you have all of that information. Be careful because, to be honest, that falls under your perception. Therefore, have an open mind when doing this.

Listening is key in gaining any type of true Knowledge for Wisdom and Understanding to develop. Those elements will be key once you have become the individual you have been working to become because there will be traps and slips a normal eye can't see.

Learn (Understand):

Until you can truly Look (Observe) and Listen (not Hear) you won't be able to reap the rewards of Learning or Understanding thoroughly. The former two must precede the latter or there is no completeness to it. I don't claim to wholly understand something until I have dissected the subject at hand from every angle I can conjure up and have battle-tested my conclusion with other intelligent minds.

The bible even says in Proverbs "In all thy getting, get understanding." Proverbs is said to have had most of it written by the wisest man that roamed the planet, King Solomon. Therefore it would be wise to listen to his instructions. Some people may think "Why is having an "Understanding" so important?" I've often made decisions without having that part because I didn't know how profound an impact the ignorance of a situation could have on my turn out. I'll tell you a few things that Understanding grants you when moving forward in life.

1. Full information before moving forward.

-       When you're making a move it's always best to know the essentials that are necessary to have success.

2.   Empathy is accessible.

-       When you can fully understand what a person is going through at the time you have the ability to empathize with them to a degree because you've figuratively stepped into their shoes.

3.   Great judgment.

-       You will be able to make rational decisions based on facts and thorough information which will allow you to make an unbiased judgment.

Remember Where You Came From

In 2017 I was "introduced" to a great mind that would change my perspective on things forever and ultimately propel me to go after the levels I move towards now without fear. I say introduced, however, we never formally met it was more of his mind that I had a chance to sit with and allow to guide me.

That great man was Nipsey Hussle and I met him through his music and later, after being released, I studied his walk via interviews, videos, quotes, etc. To this day I maintain his "Marathon

Continues" Mentality when pursuing my endeavors. My children's mom even gifted me with a portrait of him I have hanging in the room that I wake up and talk to set myself for the day. That may sound extreme but when you come from a broken home with absolutely no direct male figures to look up to you set your standards low and allow whoever is willing into your mind. That's how I started in my gangbanging career, lost and hopeless looking for guidance. Therefore, later in my life, looking for substance, I was blessed with an individual like Nipsey therefore I took it and ran with it to the fullest.

Mind you, I was a bit biased with Nipsey when I first heard him rap back in 2012. He was a Crip and where I'm from they were the enemies. I gave him half a listen and was like "he's cool for a crip" then left him alone. Ironically, years later after I had overcome those limitations in thinking, it was a hoover (our most hated rivals) that actually told me to listen to Nipsey again and I obliged.

The charisma in his voice when he said "Let me show you N***** how I came up. Similar to climbing out the grave huh?" had me like 'Hell yeah' I feel you let's get out this grave and become something. Or how I could understand him when he rhymed "I'm gone take it there, this time around I'm gone make it clear. I spoke some things into the universe and they appeared. I'll say it's worth it, I won't say it's fair. Find your purpose or you're wasting air."

However some of the lines that struck me the deepest were his humblest. They ultimately altered my perspective on the streets, my success later in life, and how to relate the two. "Laces in my blue Chucks, represent my bro's first. Staring at this rolly bezzy while I soul search." What he was saying is despite all of his success he still represents where he came from and what he saw. You can almost argue the point that his authenticity and loyalty to his roots ultimately got him murdered. However, his legacy will live forever because he was Humble and never forgot the streets that he struggled in.

When I listened to that particular song in 2019 I was on my way out of prison it altered my perspective. Up until then, I battled with myself about separating my success and "new self" from the guys or territories that I grew up around. The goal was to get big and get as far away from everybody and everything that reminded me of my past in general. Nipsey showed me that that isn't the goal. The goal is to reach your highest levels, reach back and help those who want it directly but don't forget those who don't know they need it.

Now I'm not saying that you engulf yourself in the same activities and hang around the same haunts you struggled in, that would be detrimental to what you built everything for. I'm saying that you don't forget those places and the people who you may have left behind. Find ways to help them help themselves and your legacy will be written in stone.

Friends/Family

I once heard Jay-Z say that, "When you reach those high levels of success it's important to have people around you that knew you before you became big because they can keep you grounded." The motivational speaker Lisa Nichols also said the same thing in one of her speeches about how to maintain your old friends and also mingle in new groups.

Those tidbits of wisdom forced me to re-analyze my current circle. It's a mix of business owners, professionals, and what I call "Graduated Gang Members." What I mean by a graduated gang member is they are someone who went through the course of the streets however have made it out to tell the story and elevated to new heights aside from that. They never disowned their neighborhood, nor have I, however they don't direct their energy in a negative form like they use to.

Those former gang members have probably taught me more about life than any of the business owners or professional friends have because the gang members understand my past. Therefore, they can help me navigate in the present with my somewhat altered mind. That's not to take credit away from my other friends because they have taught me a lot about family, love, finances, etc. things that many of us who come from the streets struggle with. It's simply those from the street keep me in the understanding that I have to keep moving forward because I'm always only one mismove away from slipping back into the crowded caprices filled with weed smoke and hot pistols. A nightmare I never want to go back to.

All in all, it's important to be humble enough not to get big-headed when you reach these new levels in life. Especially not to the point where the people who were with you before are treated like bull poop. Not everyone can go to the top with you, that must be understood. However, everyone should not be left at the bottom either. Some stuck it out with you in the trenches of life. Those trenches didn't have to be the streets, it could have been when you lost your job and couldn't take care of yourself or the family. It could have been when you lost a close relative or friend and couldn't contain yourself emotionally. Whatever the case may be, it doesn't matter how unsuccessful or how much of an underachiever that friend is to you. As long as they aren't trying to tear down what you have created. If someone was with you at your worst bring them with you at your best or you're undeserving of what you have been blessed to experience.

Environment

Another thing we tend to do is reach these levels of success, get as far away from where we come from, and forget about it. Although we may remain in contact with the people, we disconnect from the place. I experienced this situation and I hadn't even reached any level of success yet worth moving around for. I figured that it would be dangerous and a waste of time to visit my old neighborhood because the game had changed and the players were different, creating an unstable environment in which I had no interest.

However, I still could remember the joy of sitting with my past homeboys, some who were now deceased due to the streets; others doing "forever dates" in prison, and thinking "Man I miss that day." Not the chaos of looking out for a rival gang member to harm or come looking for us, but the times where it was just laughter and enjoyment of being in the presence of each other celebrating the fact we were still alive today because tomorrow we may not be. Those moments were serene and to this day I still hold dear to my heart. Many of those memories piled up and led me to visit the projects I started in and eventually to the hood I claim.

I grew up in the Yesler Terrace Projects which used to be one of the poorest projects in Seattle, Wa. The thing is people think that the entire Seattle is filled with wealth. However, they haven't seen the projects or poor parts that are ignored and co-exist with the people who have money. Anyways, I stayed there until I was fourteen years old and my grandmother went to prison (I'll explain that in another book). When I left the Terrace I had pretty much left it for good especially since I had started hanging out with a new crowd up the street in the Central District. I got with a small group of kids and we were given the "Keys" (Go Ahead) by the older gangsters in the neighborhood to pioneer the next generation of Cherry Street. That entire journey is a story in itself before I ended up at 22 years old facing life in prison. After the sentence, I felt I was never going back to either neighborhood. I would build my success and stay away from the past in general.

Later on, as a free man, I realized that the neighborhood was as much of my story as my journey growing out of it. Therefore, I decided to visit both the Yesler Terrace and the Central District. When I saw my old projects again after 5 years and some change it was mind-blowing. The entire place was redone and everyone I had grown up with was either no longer there or living in a renovated looking place. However, I went up the street to a part that hadn't been touched yet and saw all of the Graffiti, trash laying around, and old chipped paint. That made me feel at home again. I felt that it was a lot tinier than I once remembered. Looking at the area I didn't know how I comfortably maneuvered around when I was younger but I loved it. So many old memories flooded back into my mind and honestly, I was humbled. For some strange reason, I found myself missing some of the struggles while at the same time maintaining a sense of gratitude for how far I had come.

The next stop was the Central District, now that was a little more tricky. The "C.D." had experienced the power of gentrification yet there was still a lot of madness hanging around. It was a far more dangerous terrain and although I once navigated through it I wasn't familiar with all of the current players. Nonetheless, I felt as if it was my obligation to go and see the hood.

When I pulled up on 28th and Jackson my heart immediately started to pick up and those instincts I had from the streets kicked in full throttle. There were dudes on that corner that I had exchanged bullets with, others I had fought, and then more I had never met. To top it off there was an uneasy feeling of 'who's going to make the first move' in which I had not planned on doing in the first place. However, those who knew me and who I used to be were nervous as to what type of energy I was bringing and not in a scared way more out of caution because they were heavily involved in the streets as well.

I shook hands with those I knew and those I knew didn't like me. The energy I felt after leaving was dark and palpable to the point I felt icky. The individuals on the block were really like zombies. My brothers in arms at one point had lost all life. They were either extremely overweight and out of shape or malnourished and super skinny. You could smell the smoke, cheap alcohol, and must on many of them. Their hair was unkempt and the thing is they were cool with it.

However, the fact that humbled me is that only five years and some change prior I was the same way with my hair nappy, drinking 211 beers, baggy clothes, and busted shoes, still feeling like that guy because I'd kill you for nothing. The gun gave me the power I figured in my mind. Seeing my brothers of the struggle really struggling while I had ascended to a different platform to some degree really gave me an experience of humility. I knew then that if I fell back asleep and stopped grinding for mines then all would be lost and much would be wasted. My decision was made that day not to put myself in that situation again unless I was there to cause some sort of change and bring some help. Besides that, I would keep to my new life and build success.

Hidden Jewel

One thing I didn't notice until now was that by going back to my old neighborhood I was also addressing my fear. There had been plenty of times in life where I had gotten myself incarcerated, said I would change, then went back to the neighborhood to repeat the same cycle all over again. Today I see that the fear was repeating that cycle and therefore I made the neighborhood my enemy. In my mind, that place is what always brought me back to the disaster.

Let me tell you this now my friend. It doesn't matter Where or Who you change unless you change your own way of thinking. Everything that will manifest itself outside has to come from within. Remember that when you're deciding who or what it is that keeps causing you to fail.

The Results

You will come to find that humility will open doors that arrogance never could and would probably close. I truly believe that until I humbled myself it wasn't profound growth. By "Profound Growth" I mean that growth that comes from the inside out. It may start in your soul, up to your mind, and out into the outer world. The growth that comes otherwise is something you may wear because you read a bunch of books and may even hang around a lot of smart people who make you look even smarter. Trust me it isn't real, well let me say it isn't as effective as having it start from within.

People will want to form more solid relationships with you because you don't make them feel smaller or like they have to "Come up to your level" to talk to you. More students seem to attract to the teacher who will sit down with them rather than stand over them. You will also learn a lot more because by being humble you find that you tend to listen more with an understanding that you don't know it all.

Small things like the sight of a team of ants carrying off leaves to their nest will become huge to you because humility breeds an appreciation for spectacles like that.

All in all, being a humble individual in this world will serve you well in so many different facets of life that it is disabling not to be. Point out the great attributes of others before yourself. Look, Listen, and Learn from everything and everyone around you. Then in all of your growing never forget where you came from. Not just the physical neighborhood you grew up in but from the place where you started at which will always keep you grounded.

<u>What's Your Next Move?</u>

1.   What are one of your flaws that you didn't notice you've had until now?

2.   Who in your circle actually has that as a strength? (Point that out to them.)

3.   What are you going to do to make sure you Look, Listen, and Learn moving forward?

4.   Where did you start in life? If you haven't begun moving then where are you going or want to be?

Jewel #8: Trust The Process

" Trust the process. We always end up right where we need to be, right when we're meant to be there."

-        Unknown

October 6, 2020, I had finished my prison bid and successfully made it through a re-entry program that let me out six months early on house arrest. It was now time for me to begin my new life officially without any limitations to my freedom except for an occasional check in with my department of corrections officer. All in all, things were about to be great because I was about to begin a new journey of freedom and positivity in my life.

Now, am I saying that everything went as I planned being released from prison.....Hell No.

1.   I figured by the time I was off of home monitoring I'd be making at least $60,000 a year and starting my own business. However, I was laid off from my job for reasons outside of my control, and though I had legally started my business the lack of structure was harming its growth potential.

2.   Thought some people that I reconnected with would be inspired by my evolution and ask me how they could do it too and follow my lead...yeah right. Instead, half the time when I reached out they didn't answer or the other half they pretended to listen to what I had to say only to change the subject and go back to what they knew me as. Those responses caused us to move further from each other than we already were.

3.   My children's mother and I rode the majority of time behind bars out together. Even after my ex-girlfriend left me for dead, my child's mother stepped up and held things down when she didn't have to.

In my mind, we were set to be married and I could "fix" whatever we had that was broken. Yeah, we both learned a lot there. We decided to split up after I was released and those who knew us understood but outside of that I looked like the monster. Our kids, her parents, friends, etc. all looked at me with bias and I understand why but wish they'd have taken the time to gain an understanding.

Those are just three of the things that come directly to mind that didn't pan out how I planned it. The world had changed more than I thought it had. The man I became in prison had to learn how to transition into the man in the world which was difficult in its own way. I made mistakes I said I would never make again and things were just all over the place for a moment.

Look, I can go on and on if I want to about what didn't go as planned. However, through all of this, I learned to trust the process. In the rest of this chapter, I'm going to break down those three major changes and how it was all a part of the process that was supposed to happen although I didn't see it like that in the beginning. Please pick up what jewels you can and enjoy the lessons.

The Middle

An unknown wise individual once quoted "Procrastination is the enemy of success." I agree with that statement wholeheartedly and the reason I do is that it has destroyed so much of my potential success and I've also been able to watch others lose out due to procrastination. I once sat down and talked with my cellmate, Big Phil. Phil was a hefty guy but had extreme swagger but on top of all that he was like a genius. He was a hustler to the soul and his mind was that of Harvard students. The man could take two drops of water and sell it to you for the price of a gallon making you feel like it was right.

Anyways he and I would sometimes sit around and talk past mistakes and money moves. One day he told me how his goal before getting locked up was to touch a million dollars and he had it step by step planned out. However, he had another friend who was already in the business world come and talk to him about an investment that was about to increase in value tenfold. Phil is a smart guy who knew that it sounded rational but he already had his money planned for the million-dollar move. His friend kept telling him bro I put my money in this cryptocurrency called "Bitcoin" if you buy in now for a few hundred you could get a whole bunch and be rich when it spikes. Phil knew the truth but decided to wait on it. Phil said "Bro, do you know I got locked up and that shit went past 10,000 dollars. With what I had to invest I would have made millions. Instead, I lost the million-dollar plan and the million-dollar opportunity because I decided to wait."

That really resonated with me because I have always been an avid procrastinator. In my mind, there would always be another day for another chance. I'm here to tell you now that thinking that there is always tomorrow is the biggest most arrogant assumption you can make about life just go ahead and ask the people who died last night.

I say all of that to attack the "Why" behind the reason we often procrastinate to move on things. My personal belief is that there are three parts to any task or journey were going to embark on. There's 'The Beginning (Where You Are), The End (Where You Want To Be), and The Middle (The Stuff You Gotta Go Through To Get There). The beginning isn't what scares us because we're already there I mean how much worse could it get. The end won't put fear in us because that's the goal it should actually motivate us. It's that Damn middle. The middle is unknown. It's like standing on one side of a swamp and the other side is freedom yet you see that the only way to get across is through these murky, dirty, potentially alligator-infested waters. That's what truly scares you about the middle.

Now, being so worried about what could go on in "The Middle" we freeze up and don't move at all. There's a fear that it could be the wrong choice or to put in real-world terms, "He may be the wrong choice." There's the belief that whatever in there will eat you alive or "I can't compete with them they're better than I am." All sorts of self-defeating doubts may arise to prevent you from moving forward. However, this is where people are made into Successes or Failures. Those who strap up their bootlaces and hop in and keep going through blindly navigating through the BS win. Those who stay stuck deciding on how or if they should move forward lose, simple as that.

How To Get In and Move in the Middle:

1.   Juuuuuuump!

Look, in my opinion, there are two types of people in this world when it comes to facing challenges. Those who rise and those who fall. Now, just because they fall doesn't mean they never get to the challenge they just crawl in at a slow comfortable pace. Those who rise just eye things and hop in the fire.

I'm the latter of the two people. I like to hop in and trust my instincts and prowess to help me learn enough on the way to be successful. In my experience, not just personally either, I've seen far more people who just hopped in and learned on foot prosper more than their crawling counterparts. The ones who jump just have more oomph behind them to succeed and seem almost blind to their fears putting odds on their side.

When I first started my online clothing business Manifest Apparel I didn't know anything about selling clothes ESPECIALLY online. I was on house arrest coming off of a five-plus year prison bid for God's sake. However, I wanted to have my words of motivation inside of every closet and to monetize my skills therefore, I saved up 200 dollars, came up with designs, sent them to someone to make, and bam they were finished. Honestly, it wasn't something that I saw as a business initially more like a public service. The way people began buying from me and liked the concept turned it into a business and mistake after mistake helped me figure things out.

Now, if I told you how many people let me know they had been "thinking about selling clothes" after I got going your ears would bleed. These people had been out for years and some had never even been incarcerated and here I am two months out doing this and getting asked advice on how to start an apparel business. That's the main difference between the "Jumpers" and the "Crawlers", one goes in and gets it done while the other waits and misses the opportunity.

The latter usually gets the bag while the other is left picking up scraps.

If you're reading this book it means you support my movement and success in some way and I don't want you to pick up the scraps. I encourage you to stop doubting, self-criticizing, crying, and Jump!!! It will be the only way to get that bag and trust that you will figure the rest out on the way.

2. Swim

Now, that you've said "F" it to that stupid little voice in your head that holds you back with fear and jumped into the mix we have to get you going or you'll run back. We may tend to think that once we've got past the ledge and are in the thick of things we're in the clear because at least we started, but that's not true. Getting started is a small piece of the end game but it's extremely important.

The next point is to swim. You ever see a competing swimmer jump into the water and freeze up because it's cold, the waters too deep, or whatever else excuse there is to use in the book? No, they jump in headfirst and the last thing you see is their feet pedaling them to their destination. Now, if you look at people who are not competitive and just want to jump in the water to overcome some types of fear you'll notice that when they do they freeze up immediately when the water engulfs their body in its low temperature. They weren't ready for all of that it was just to overcome fear and either they'll hop back out since their mission is accomplished or they'll get to swimming and carry on. Whatever the case DON'T FREEZE UP!

The point I'm trying to make is once you jump into fulfilling your goal-attack it aggressively. Don't let up on your pursuit. You must be the lion and that goal or goals must be your antelope. If you don't succeed you don't eat type of mentality. One arm in front of the other is all you should be thinking about while looking ahead towards where you are trying to go. Nothing to the left or the right of you should be a distraction at all. No friends, significant other, family not nobody! All you're worried about is swimming through this B.S. to get where you need to get to.

Also, keep swimming! Some sharks cannot stop swimming or they will die because they'll lack the oxygen-rich waters passing their gills to keep them alive. That is true for you as well. If you get in there swimming then stop for whatever reason all of the momentum, confidence, and affirmations that were feeding you initially will cease and cause you to drown. Therefore, you must keep moving no matter how tough it gets even if you're not seeing the results you want right away. You must keep that end game in mind to make it to the other side. Since we're speaking of the other side, let's get into one of the biggest downsides of victory.

3.   Turn Around, Then Never Look Back

In 'Phillipians 3:13' the Apostle Paul speaks to the church saying "Brothers and sisters I do not consider myself to have yet taken ahold of it. But one thing I do: Forgetting what is behind and straining towards what is ahead..." he continues to talk about pressing towards the goal. Initially, when I read that verse I thought I fully understood what he was talking about. In my understanding, he meant that he left his mistakes in the past and pressed towards a better future which was the goal, easy. If that's what you got out of it then kudos because at the same time it isn't necessarily wrong. However, allow me to broaden your perspective a bit.

In what other ways can we get stuck looking in our past? Does it only have to be a guilty feeling because of poor decision making? Are there any other reasons? Maybe a past love we lost? Or maybe someone we loved has passed away and we feed on their memories. But, what else could there be? Is there a chance that we can look back at something that excites us and fills us up with pride and confidence if only for the moment? What could give us that feeling? How about ACCOMPLISHMENTS?

I remember one morning in my prison cell watching T.D. Jakes brings up this Philippians scripture and he broke it down in a new way for me. He said that Apostle Paul had already been saved and had at this point racked up a bunch of miracles under his belt and had people who both loved and hated him already. He could have lived the rest of his life on his past victories and accomplishments for God. However, he chose not to and said 'Forgetting what is behind me...' he was pressing forward. That is a difficult skill to develop however it will bring you so much more success and humble you at the same time. Once I was enlightened to what he truly meant I stopped hanging up my certificates on the wall so I wouldn't be captured by that. In my head, I had to grind like I was still at the bottom trying to change. That scripture changed my whole perspective on victory.

For you, once you're in the water swimming and have made it past the Doubts, Fears, Ridicule, etc. it could be extremely tempting to celebrate once you're on land. You may hop on the solid ground turn around with your arms up like Rocky Balboa, jump around all over the place, do a dance, etc. etc. Then before you know it it's dark and you've lost your way again because you can no longer see what's in front of you. Not only is there a probability you'll get lost again trying to feel around the dark jungle but who's lurking in the night to make you prey at this point. Now, that's just speaking figuratively but there are a lot of people who get a few victories and sit there staring at them so long they lose sight of the next move. Look at the one-hit wonders in music it's all over after they aren't catchy anymore. Look at the sports stars that get all that money and don't plan for their next move, they end up broke trying to get on some reality t.v. show. Don't be those guys. Forget what is behind and keep pressing towards the Goals.

Appreciate Every Moment, Watch The Future

People see me as crazy when I reminisce on some parts of prison or I tell them about a certain situation I miss. Things like waking up in the morning to my goofy celly "Gooey" (Won't explain the name lol) drinking his tea watching television and I'd make my coffee turn on some country music videos and talk stuff to him all morning. Things like that feeling I used to get when I saw my kid's mom and the little ones coming in for a visit and my heart would skip a beat but for some reason, we couldn't recapture those feelings when I was released which led to our break up. Basically growing up in the system from juveniles to prisons I recall memories that hold such sentimental value over me it's disturbing to the point at one time I thought I may have been institutionalized. However, I began to realize that some of those moments were actually great snapshots of life despite the circumstances. There are dudes in there doing time ranging from 3 years to life without parole who I may never see again but made cherishable memories with that will bind us forever. No matter you gotta respect that.

The ability to cherish the moment may have been instilled in me from growing up in an environment where one day you could be slap boxing with your friend and the next he or she is being picked up off the ground by the paramedics deceased to gunshot wounds. Maybe it came from having so many people exit my life from a young age and learning to appreciate them while they're still here. Whatever it may be I learned to cherish the moment through hardships that are extremely important to do. However, what I didn't learn until later on in my life when all of this criminal stuff was going on was to 'Watch the future.'

Growing up, although we learned to enjoy the time we had with each other because we were dying so fast, we never looked at the future like "What if we do somehow survive?" Therefore, as we aged and beat statistics to a degree we were never properly prepared for what came next. Finances weren't taught to us. Owning your own home was like a different language. Even taking care of kids that we helped create wasn't a part of the "Plan". There was just never a thought to plan.

The ability to look towards the future was developed after facing the rest of my future in a prison cell. That was my large wake-up call. I hadn't planned for anything up until that point and the situation I was in wasn't a part of my plan, maybe theirs but not mines. I had fallen into someone else plans by not having my own. Once I realized that I swore to never ignore my future again. Therefore, I paired the two skills "Appreciate the moment" but I keep my eye on the Future Always. Let's talk about this.

There are usually two types of people that are put on this earth and the third, in my opinion, is self-made. The first type is what we'll call the "in the moment" person and the next we'll call the "Think ahead" individual.

The Moment Person:

See, the one who is solely focused on living in the moment catches

every beautiful detail of what's happening now, giving them the ability to

really respect the times. They harp on the fact that tomorrow has

enough worry for itself and we should all focus on doing what we have to

do right now to survive or make it. There isn't necessarily a problem being

this type of person if you're okay with addressing issues as they come

and enjoying as well as dealing with what's happening now. For some,

that style of living actually brings much peace and joy in life.

My kid's mother is a person who really focuses on the moment. Her philosophy was that she has to deal with what's going on now as opposed

to trying to secure the future. I get it but I never truly agreed with it. The

reason being is that with that mentality it seemed as if she was

constantly having to put out fires that may have been avoided had she of

only looked a little further ahead.

　　The thing is when you choose to live exclusively in the moment you'll

miss out on planning for your future or protecting yourself against what's

coming. Imagine if our great leaders only lived in the moment without

planning and building for the future. We would all be in a much worse

position. I see this type of thinking when I look at some of my old peers

both dead and alive. I myself lived under this mentality for a long time as well. We often didn't plan far into the future because we were unsure if

we'd live to see tomorrow in the first place. A lot of us didn't live to see

that day either. However, those of us who got lucky enough to breathe

today's air ended up underprepared for life because we didn't plan for it.

Whenever you don't plan for the life you leave a vacuum that is likely to be

filled by anything at that point. For some of us, it was drugs and others

took up sex or alcohol. For me, it ended up being all sorts of crime and

ultimately prison. The point I'm getting at is that living exclusively in and

for the moment didn't get me anywhere but unprepared for what was to

come.

The Think Ahead Person:

After the many disputable things I laid out about the one who decides to stay in the moment or day to day grind, you'd think I was myself in favor of thinking ahead all of the time. Wrong! However, I'll lay out the most agreeable attributes of someone who lives in the future.

I will attest that a great thing future dwellers do is plan. By that skill alone they can avoid a fire even starting and if it already has they can put it out before it becomes large or prepare for the safety measures if it must be embraced. Also, when I say "fires" I mean the circumstances that arise only when there is opposition to living the average life. These fires only come to burn down establishments that test the status quo and threaten to be a successful thing. In other words, if you're not experiencing any resistance then you're not doing enough. Therefore, embrace those fires as success points. The forward thinkers are great at seeing these ahead of time and adjusting if need be.

Another great attribute with thinking into the future is that having a plan for your vision actually brings a sense of comfort because you know that there is a blueprint for you to follow on your way to success. Therefore, if things do sort of knock you off your pivot you know that many other things still need to be done anyways to get after what you're getting at around that time. Planning is probably the strongest skill someone who lives in the future has and it's something we all should actually strive for when pursuing success.

Those are only a couple of the favorable things the future thinkers bring to the table. Their strongest attribute is planning. However, I have to sting them as I also did the Moment heads. Thinking in the future is, but if you go too far and stay too long you lose touch with what's happening at the moment that could affect that future. Say that you're planning to expand your business from a small place into something large and admirable. You have these strong plans, an effective blueprint, and the ambition to put the work in. However, in all your planning for the future, you've forgotten to check in on the current state of your employees who feel as if they are being neglected and left out of the big picture. They are beginning to feel insecure about their positions in the job and almost mistreated. Some are planning to leave and they are slowly convincing the others to follow suit. Before you know it you spend all of this time and money to move forward into your vision but you look back and see you have no employees left to follow you into it.

That's just a larger example of living in the future too much and how it can affect your movement.

There's plenty of practical matters such as ignoring the truth of what something is right now by obsessing on what it probably can be later on....relationships. Or even neglecting the time with your kids because you're living in the vision of your success later on.

The Self-Made (Balance):

We now arrive at the type of person I favor the most and whom we should all strive to become more and more like every day. I consider these people self-made because to reach this level of discipline you must practice it every single moment of life and not ease up. That sounds extremely difficult, however, I promise you as it becomes a habit the process becomes more simple.

These types of people have mastered or are mastering the art of living in the moment, yet looking into the future and making their best plans, decisions, and judgment from this wisdom. Their philosophy is to be fully in the moment with plans for the future in mind. That means if you had plans to expand the business there would be a meeting with employees discussing these plans, checking on their states of minds, and focusing on if the bottom line is currently being met before moving forward to the next level. This also means living in your vision but understanding that those whom you're responsible for right now will likely be the ones you are responsible for in the future. Therefore continuously making sure that they are good right now. The balanced individual can look into the deep forest, spot a potential fire, and come back to the tree everyone is standing at to effectively communicate the issue and how to address it.

I've been a guy for the moment and a lot of mess I wasn't prepared for has come with it. I have been an extreme future guy in prison because that's almost all you can be, and I've been let down because of it. However, after maturing in wisdom and understanding I have learned to take a more balanced approach in my business and personal life which has really been working out for the better. Out of these three types, I encourage you to become the third and see where the practice takes you.

The Final Jewel

"If you own this story, you get to write the ending."

-   Brene' Brown

As I sit here a free man editing this book with a cup of oat milk, about ready to go to the gym, looking at life with a new growth perspective, I am a proud man. Not that I haven't made many mistakes before, during, and after my incarceration. What I am proud of is the fact that I am still standing. I still have the pen in my hand writing this novel of my life where the end is unpredictable but the pages I have control over.

Everything has changed, and honestly, nothing went as planned. The only thing that did go as I predicted was the fact that I would stay strong throughout the tidal waves of life. There's individuals I see to this day whom were incarcerated with me that had so much fire and passion while inside but lost it all and burned out once they got out. Most of the time they are embarrassed to see me and attempt to hide. However, I hold no judgement over anyone because I've been that guy before.

I told you in the beginning my goal was to give you guys something that hopefully could be useful in your own lives based on how these lessons worked for me in my own. I pray there were some jewels that were useful that you can pick up and place in your treasure chest or at least share with another. It may have been a long journey but trust me if you stay down and committed to change it will happen. I know this because it happened for me. Remain mighty and focused in all of your endeavors. Until next time friends, PEACE.

Remember:

1. Do What You Have To Do…NOW
2. Figure Out Who You're Not
3. Who Do I Want To Become?
4. Be Consistent
5. Set Life Boundaries
6. Relate
7. Be Humble
8. Trust The Process

Contact Me:

Email: Manifestmservices@gmail.com (All Coaching Inquiries or Speaking Engagements)

Instagram: PersonalSuccess_Coach

FaceBook: DeVonte Ase'

Made in the USA
Las Vegas, NV
04 February 2021

17092488R00085